BARBARA HEPWORTH

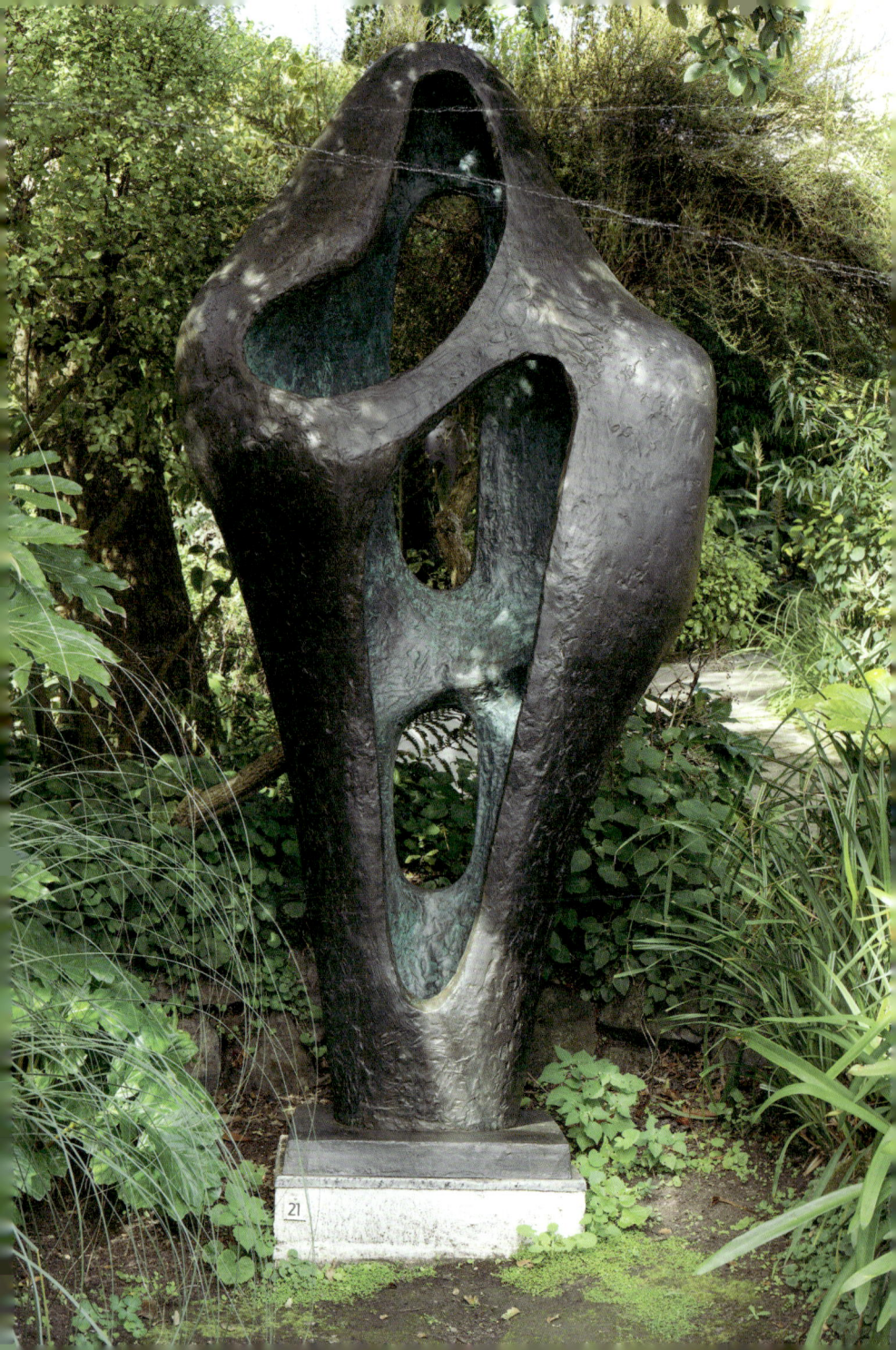

BARBARA HEPWORTH

**KATY
NORRIS**

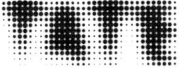

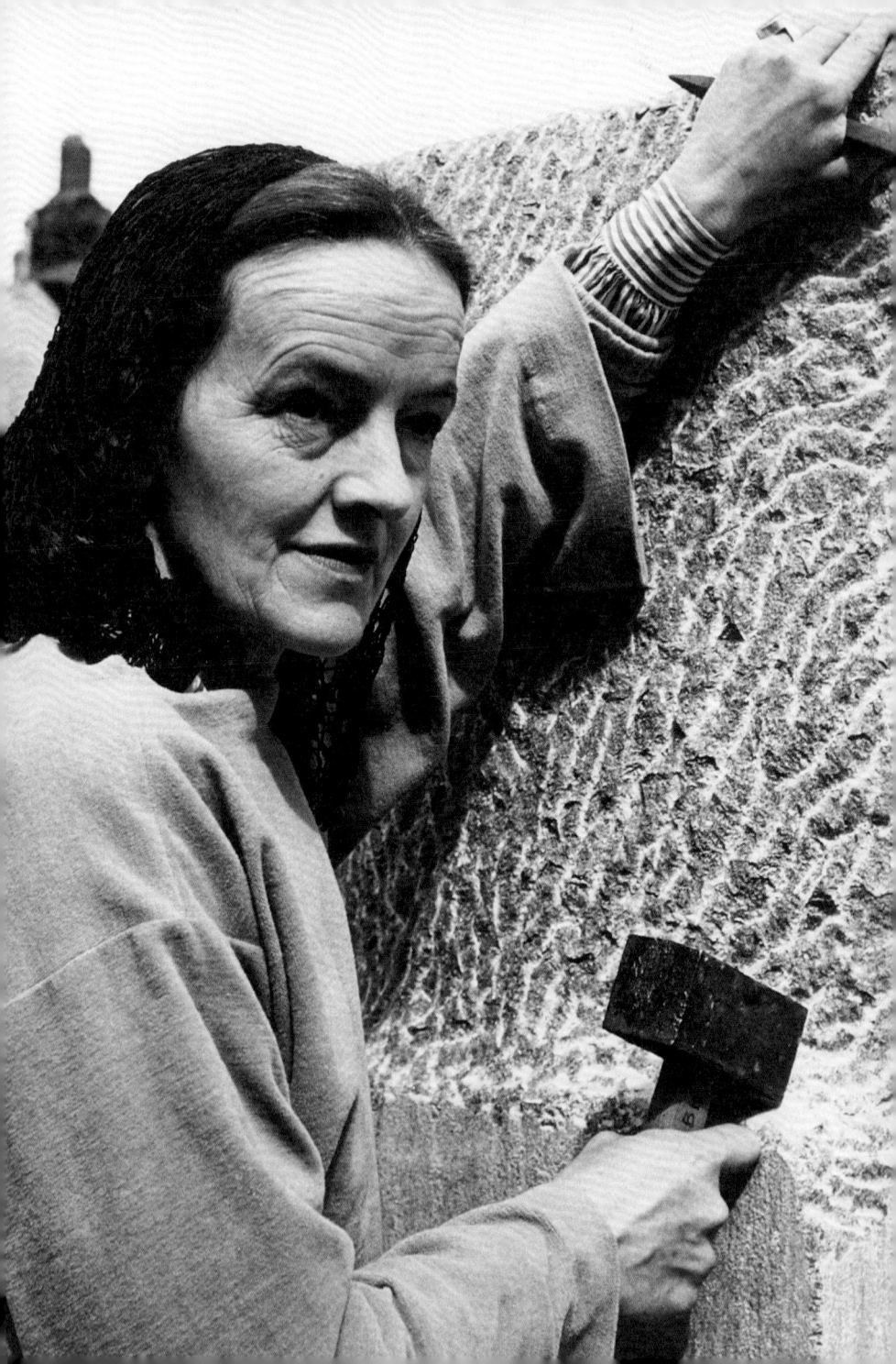

Barbara Hepworth was a leading figure in modern sculpture during the twentieth century. Her career spanned more than five decades, coinciding with a period of seismic political upheaval that encompassed the rise of fascism, global conflict and nuclear crisis. Hepworth was deeply committed to rediscovering art's civic function, and her sculptures promoted a sense of rootedness, both in nature and in our collective, social environment, providing stability in an otherwise uncertain world.

Starting out in London as a carver working exclusively with stone and wood, Hepworth turned to metal casting while living in Cornwall after the Second World War. This development proved crucial, enabling her to create monumental sculptures that won international acclaim for their powerful expressions of optimism and unity.

Despite these considerable achievements, Hepworth faced significant challenges. Her financial background was relatively modest and she relied on patrons and commercial sales to support her practice. She also battled against sexist attitudes within the art establishment. Today, the fact that she is recognised alongside male sculptors such as Henry Moore is a mark of her professional tenacity and, above all, her determination to shape public understanding of her work herself.

EARLY LIFE

Barbara Hepworth was born in Wakefield, West Yorkshire to a middle class family in 1903. Her father, Herbert Hepworth, was a civil engineer, who gradually rose to the position of county surveyor. Barbara attended a progressive independent school, Wakefield Girls' High School, winning two scholarships there in 1915 and 1917. She nurtured an early passion for ancient Egyptian art, as well as rhythm and movement through her lessons in eurythmics. The principles of mathematics and solid geometry also came easily to her, perhaps because of Herbert's vocation and her early exposure to technical drawing. Meanwhile, it was her connection to the Yorkshire landscape – forged through trips in her father's professional motor car – that determined her ambition to become a sculptor. She later recalled: 'Every hill and valley became a sculpture in my eyes, and each landscape was intrinsic in the astonishing "architecture" of the industrial Pennines which spread west, north, and south of us.'[1]

Barbara Hepworth,
photographed by
Peter Keen, 1950
Vintage bromide print
30.1 × 24.9

DIRECT CARVING

Between 1920 and 1924, Hepworth won further scholarships to study first at the Leeds School of Art and then the Royal College of Art (RCA) in London, where she was in the same cohort as Henry Moore. Both aspiring sculptors, they entered the art world at a moment of profound change within the discipline. During the previous decade, artists such as Jacob Epstein and Henri Gaudier-Brzeska, in line with the likes of Constantin Brâncuşi and Ossip Zadkine in Paris, had chosen to carve their forms directly from start to finish, rejecting the academic convention of working with stonecutters or bronze founders to translate their designs. This immediate approach was inspired by artefacts created by civilisations outside the classical European tradition, which UK artists saw in institutions such as the British Museum. Though essentially figurative, the resulting sculptures offered a stylised interpretation unlike the realistic aesthetic traditionally promoted within Western culture.

ITALY

By the time Hepworth completed her education in 1924 she had yet to define her artistic approach. This direction was clarified during a study trip she made to Italy shortly after graduating. Hepworth had been one of the final four candidates to be considered for the prestigious British School at Rome prize; although she failed to secure this funding, during her travels she became better acquainted with the winner of the award, John Skeaping. Touring Tuscany, the pair embarked on a whirlwind romance. They married in Florence before returning to Rome, where Skeaping resumed his residency at the British School.

In Italy, Hepworth was struck by the quality of light, so unlike the gloomy atmospheres in Yorkshire and London. Such luminosity, she observed, animated the stone statues she encountered. A 'chance remark' by Skeaping's carving instructor Giovanni Ardani, that marble 'changes colour under different people's hands' fed Hepworth's concept of stone as a 'living' material.[2] Turning definitively to carving, her goal was to achieve a somatic and emotional empathy with her materials by cutting away at them. She described the process as 'an understanding, almost a kind of persuasion, and above all greater co-ordination between head and hand.'[3]

When Hepworth and Skeaping returned to London in 1926 they built their profile as an artistic duo, mounting three joint exhibitions that enhanced their reputations amongst collectors and curators. The first two shows featured Hepworth's earliest carvings, which consisted predominantly of blocky female torsos, mother and child motifs, and birds and animals (below, pp.32–3). Overall, the selections demonstrated her interest in exploring the unique qualities of different stones, while the human forms in particular drew influence from ancient Greek and early Renaissance art as well as Chinese, Mesopotamian and African sculpture.

In 1928 Hepworth and Skeaping moved to the Mall Studios, a purpose-built complex in Hampstead. Their studio apartment boasted large windows which flooded the space with natural light. In 1929 Hepworth gave birth to her first child, Paul, whose presence she claimed 'developed and strengthened' her practice.[4] That year she expanded into wood carving, opting for hardwoods from Africa and Southeast Asia that required considerable strength and dexterity to cut (p.35). Engaging with wood led Hepworth to develop her most abstract sculptures to date. Her final joint exhibition with Skeaping, held in 1930 at the prominent London gallery Arthur Tooth & Sons, featured torsos that were radically simplified (p.38). In these works Hepworth's primary aim was to unlock the properties inherent in the original vertical tree-trunks,

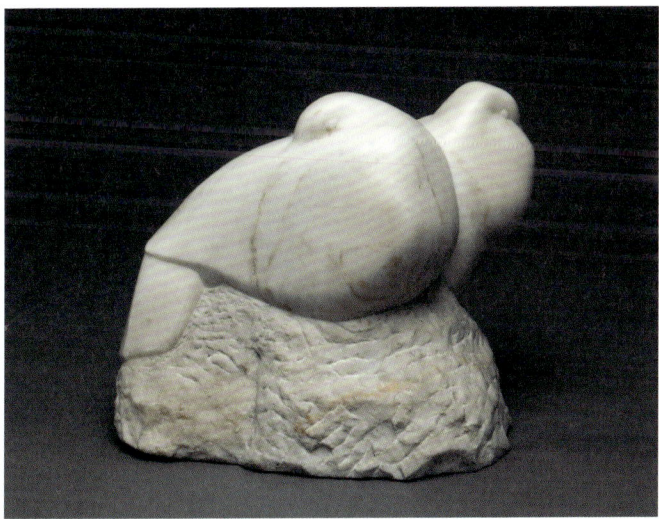

Doves (Group) 1927
Parian marble
29 × 33 × 21.5

thereby allowing the materials to determine her forms. Over the years she renegotiated this intuitive method, at other times approaching her stone block or trunk with a fully formulated concept.

Although Skeaping and Hepworth enjoyed professional successes together, their marriage faltered. Amid these difficulties Hepworth forged a new partnership with the painter Ben Nicholson, a romantic and creative union that would ultimately last just over two decades.

BEN & BARBARA

Nicholson and Hepworth were already part of the same modern art scene in London when they met in 1931. In January of that year, Nicholson and his then wife Winifred Dacre exhibited their paintings in the annual show of the Seven and Five Society, an artistic group that became more progressive under their influence. Soon afterwards Skeaping and Hepworth joined the society as permanent members, with Hepworth describing her excitement at finding a creative coalition that reflected the same simplicity and 'freedom of approach' as she was pursuing in her sculptures.[5]

That September, Nicholson joined Hepworth, Skeaping, Moore and others on a sojourn to the Norfolk coast. During the holiday he and Hepworth grew closer as their creative thirst merged with mutual adoration. She wrote to him afterwards: 'Your dear head is like the most lovely pebble ever seen and your thoughts clear as the pebbles just left by the sea'.[6] These feelings precipitated Hepworth's split from Skeaping in October 1931, followed by their amicable divorce in 1933. Meanwhile her existence intertwined artistically and emotionally with Nicholson's. In 1932 he explained: 'Barbara and I are the same… our ideas, our rhythms, our life is exactly married that we can live, think & work & move & stay still together as if we were one person.'[7]

While the profound connection between Hepworth and Nicholson was ultimately cemented by the birth of their children in 1934 and their marriage in 1938, the relationship was founded upon their common interest in modern painting and sculpture, as well as their shared spiritual beliefs. Both artists subscribed to the Christian Science theory of the 'divine' and 'mortal' mind.[8] This asserted that the 'divine mind' had the ability to perceive a genuine, harmonious existence through spiritual intuition and ultimately transcendence, while the 'mortal mind' perceived a false impression of the world based on material sensation. Grappling with this idea, Hepworth ultimately gave the same value to physical matter and bodily relationships as she did thoughts and beliefs. Nevertheless, the principle that ideas, in themselves, could generate a more perfect reality was compelling for her and Nicholson as they explored the viability of an abstract art driven as much by conceptual ideals as formal invention.

INFLUENCES FROM PARIS

In their efforts to establish a new abstract style in Britain, Hepworth and Nicholson were greatly informed by artistic movements in Paris, which was for them the epicentre of the European avant-garde. Hepworth made just ten visits to the French capital in her lifetime, but she maintained vital friendships with a rich array of sculptors, painters and designers on the continent. Throughout the early 1930s these relationships were often nurtured by Nicholson, who regularly stayed in the city.

During Easter 1933 the couple embarked on a trip to Provence, stopping at Avignon and Saint-Rémy. Initially Hepworth joined Nicholson in Paris, where they visited Brâncuşi's studio, as well as that of another leading abstract carver, Jean Arp, whose atelier was located at the edge of the Meudon forest on the outskirts of the city. Hepworth marvelled at the 'complete unity of form and material' she observed in Brâncuşi's sculptures.[9] Meanwhile, Arp's surrealist-inspired fusion of bucolic and bodily forms had a liberating effect, helping her to see 'the figure in the landscape with new eyes': 'I began to imagine the earth rising and becoming human', she later explained.[10] Returning to London from Provence via Paris and Dieppe, it was during the same trip that Hepworth visited Pablo Picasso and most likely met Georges Braque, both formative encounters that bought her into close contact with new developments in cubist painting. Of her visit to Picasso's studio she stated: 'I shall never forget the afternoon light streaming over roofs and chimney-pots through the window, on to a miraculous succession of large canvases… from which emanated a blaze of energy in form and colour.'[11]

Several of Hepworth's sculptures dating from the early 1930s reveal this exhilarating mix of influences. The larger form in *Two Heads* 1932 (p.40) recalls her description of Nicholson's features, as well as eroded pebbles she found along

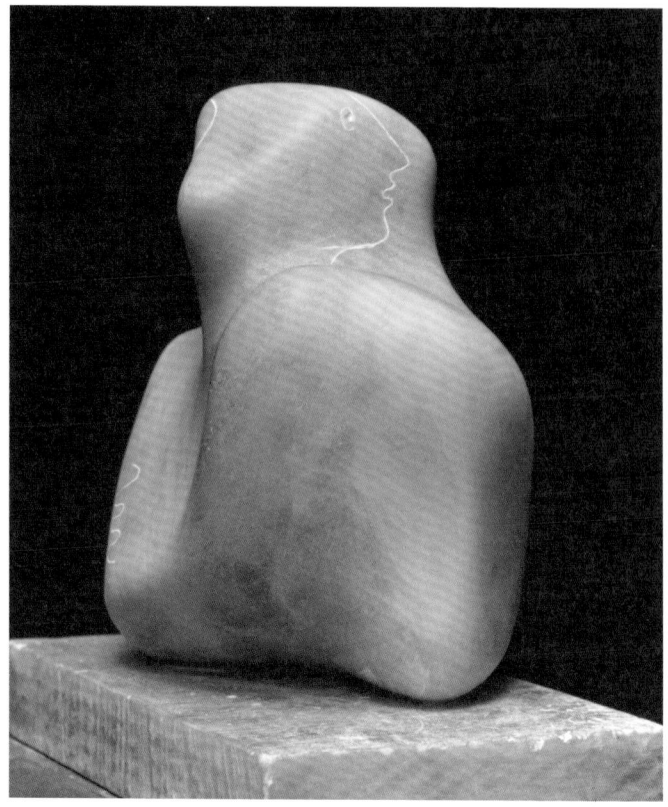

the Norfolk coastline, while *Two Forms* 1933 (p.41) incorporated two entirely separate, interlocking pieces. This arrangement has been described as 'active in a penetrative way', suggestive of the couple's physical relationship perhaps representing either 'sexual caress or sexual frustration'.[12]

The sculpture is typical of the cream alabaster carvings that Hepworth incised with anatomical details such as faces, hands and eyes. These markings seemed to float freely on the surface of her organic forms, resembling the effects of semi-abstract cubist and surrealist paintings. In another carving Hepworth delineated features that more closely resembled her own profile (above). This likeness drew inspiration from a series of self-portrait photograms that she developed following her meeting with the Hungarian photographer and painter László Moholy-Nagy, who was experimenting with the same process of creating negative shadows using light-sensitive paper (below).

Nicholson, meanwhile, reaffirmed his reciprocal interest by inscribing Hepworth's silhouette on paintings, linocut prints and hand-printed fabrics. This imagery can be seen together with Hepworth's sculptures and textile designs in photographs of the Mall Studio (p.12), which the artists shared from March 1932. Over the next two years, joint exhibitions held at Arthur Tooth and the Lefevre Gallery in London revealed their move towards abstraction – a new direction that, in general, received a lukewarm response from the British art press. However it was supported wholeheartedly by the influential critic Herbert Read, who asserted that Hepworth's sculpture was 'perfect in its freedom, its force and its contemporaneity'.[13]

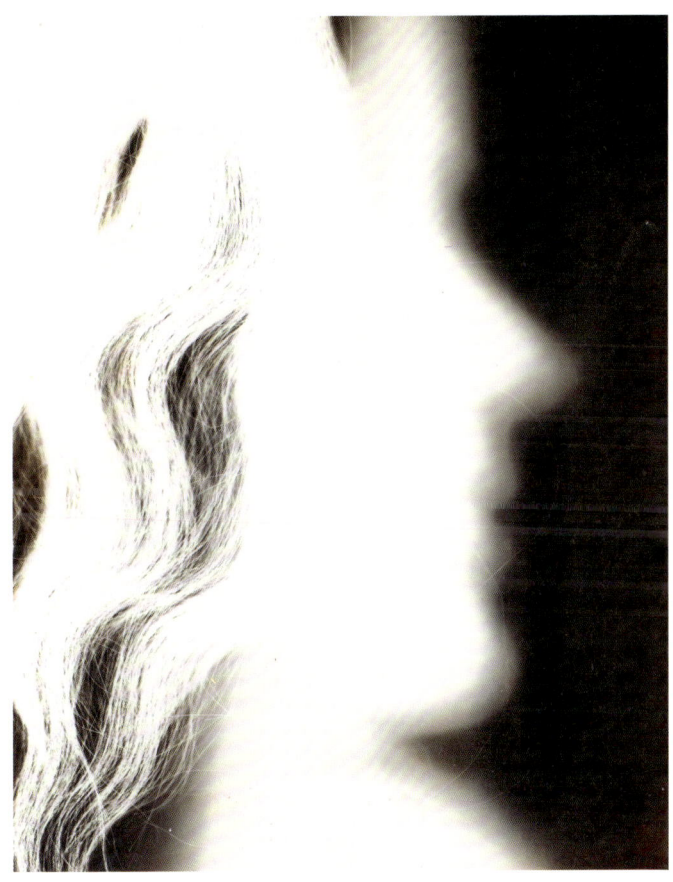

Photographs of the Mall studio, showing works by Hepworth and Ben Nicholson

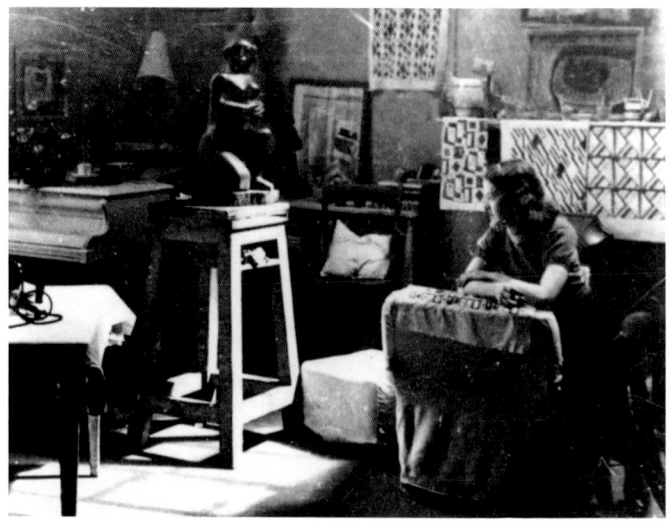

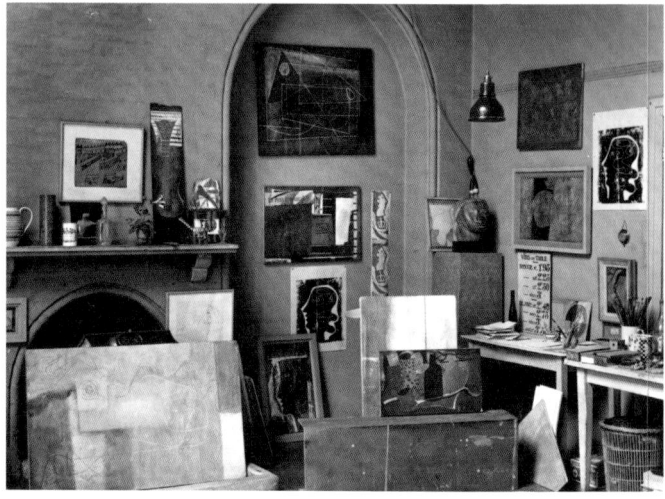

Photographs of the Mall studio, showing works by Hepworth and Ben Nicholson

A NEW SCULPTURAL ANATOMY

The exhibition at Arthur Tooth in 1932 featured Hepworth's first 'pierced' sculpture, a pink alabaster carving which she cut through with a round hole (opposite). Unlike the openings that had previously appeared in her work, which usually denoted the crook of an arm in relation to the body, here the device served a purely abstract function. It opened up her dense mass of stone to the surrounding atmosphere of light and air, thus introducing a new sense of freedom and mobility unprecedented in British sculpture. That the hole was promptly adopted by other sculptors, notably Moore, confirms the significance of this pathbreaking development. Hepworth, meanwhile, associated the piercing with her personal abstract language, which she later described as a new 'sculptural anatomy'.[14]

Negative space also constituted an important element in the evolution of Hepworth's multipart compositions. She began to trial dynamics between two differently sized forms, the smaller fitting neatly into the voids produced by the larger piece. Initially, these sculptures had some grounding in nature. Several examples were executed in the first half of 1934, during Hepworth's second pregnancy, and can therefore be interpreted as symbolic representations of the maternal bond she experienced. Indeed, in works entitled *Mother and Child* (pp.42, 43), she guided the viewer to read her forms as mother

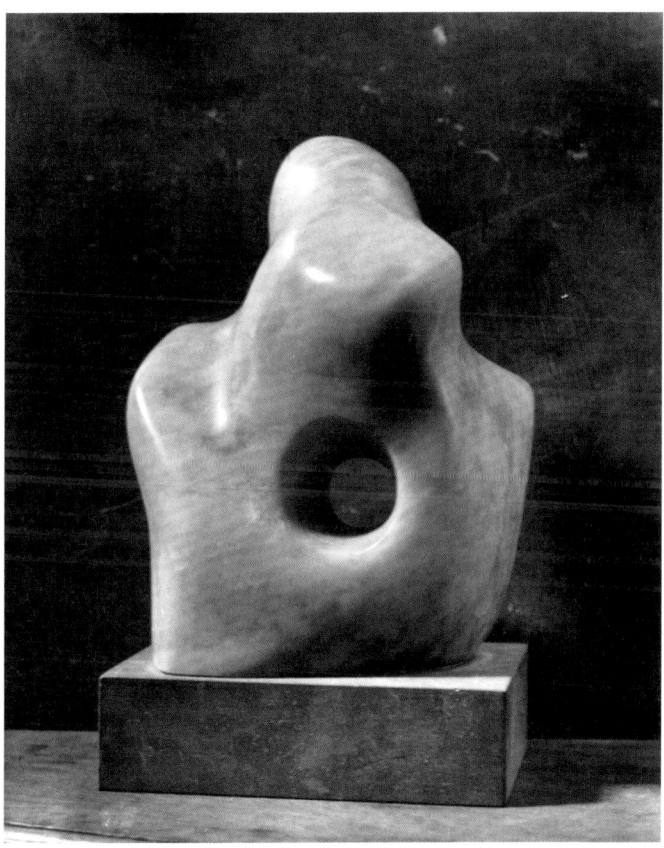

Pierced Form 1932
Pink alabaster (destroyed in the war)
25.4 high

and baby, the infant form safely 'held' by the bigger, nurturing element.

In October of that year Hepworth gave birth to not one but three babies. In the following months, while she and Nicholson became acquainted with the individualities of their triplets, their presence seemed to have the opposite effect on her sculpture: as Hepworth later described, when she returned to carving again in November, a generalised abstraction had taken root in her work. 'All traces of naturalism had disappeared', she reflected, 'although the only fresh influence had been the arrival of the children.'[15] By 1935 she had refined the individual components in *Mother and Child* to simple ovoids, now set upon a rectangular base and carved in white marble to accentuate their purity of form (p.45).

More than ever, Hepworth was concerned with the connection between solid masses and their surroundings, a synergy that was determined by their exact size, shape, texture and spatial positioning. Still, she recognised how such arrangements might continue to suggest human relationships. Reduced to their 'absolute essence', her sculptural compositions now distilled the fundamental 'quality' of such social interactions.[16]

INTERNATIONAL ABSTRACTION VS TOTALITARIANISM

As she was developing her approach to abstraction, Hepworth was also building professional networks that enriched her ideas. In Britain she and Nicholson joined Unit One, a progressive alliance of sculptors, painters and architects that embraced surrealism and abstraction, while at the same time they contributed to the Paris-based group Abstraction-Création.

Abstraction-Création was established to represent the broad church of non-representational art in Europe, but it oriented towards austere types. Members included the Russian constructivist Naum Gabo – who advocated for a utilitarian, abstract art in the service of a revolutionary society – and Piet Mondrian and Theo van Doesburg, both proponents of the Dutch movement De Stijl which established a visual language of refined geometry and primary colours.

When Hepworth visited Mondrian's Parisian studio in 1935 she described the experience as 'being transported to a new world'.[17] More broadly, the tenets of international abstraction, with its revolutionary, utopian-socialist roots, fed back into the

British art world via such initiatives as Axis, the journal of abstract art edited by Myfanwy Evans, which illustrated several of Hepworth's white marble carvings. In 1936 Evans aided the art historian Nicolete Gray in organising *Abstract and Concrete*, a UK touring exhibition that showed Hepworth, Nicholson and Moore in dialogue with many of their international peers.

Solidarity between avant-garde groups in Britain and France was forged in response to the rise of fascist dictatorships in continental Europe. Eventually many artists fled Paris for London, some finding refuge in Hampstead, close to Hepworth's studio: Gabo, Mondrian and Moholy-Nagy settled there, as did Moholy-Nagy's former colleagues from the Bauhaus school, the architect Walter Gropius and the furniture designer Marcel Breuer. Hepworth recalled that the capital became the locus of an international modernist movement committed to promoting liberal social ideals through an interdisciplinary approach to abstraction and the arts. She explained: 'Because of the danger of totalitarianism and impending war all of us worked the harder to lay strong foundations for the future through an understanding of the true relationship between architecture, painting and sculpture.'[18]

CIRCLE & CONSTRUCTIVE ART

In Britain, this collective atmosphere of creative and political idealism was articulated most clearly with the publication of *Circle: International Survey of Constructive Art* (1937), which was edited by Gabo, Nicholson and the architect Leslie Martin, alongside Hepworth and Sadie Speight as designers. Featuring statements by scientists, engineers and educationalists in addition to leading practitioners in painting, sculpture, design and architecture, the survey's purpose was to root the potentially obscure formal qualities of constructive art in measurable areas of human existence. Meanwhile, the editors communicated the social potential of an international abstract movement that could oppose oppressive fascist rhetoric.

In her text Hepworth described constructive sculpture as the 'plastic extension of thought' and argued that the principles it embodied regarding imaginative liberty were relevant to all people, writing: 'This is no escapism, no ivory tower, no isolated pleasure in proportion and space – it is an unconscious manner of expressing our belief in a possible life.'[19]

During the year of *Circle's* publication, Hepworth worked on a series that gave form to her utopian ideals (p.50). These carvings interrogated a format that was key to her practice going forward: the *Single Form*, a towering column which developed from her earlier torsos and came to represent universal human rights and freedoms. Hepworth's progressivism was underlined when a plaster from the series featured in an exhibition of cutting-edge abstract art in Paris. Yet she also associated her *Single Form* motif with ancient standing stones such as the Neolithic complex at Stonehenge, photographs of which accompanied her essay in *Circle*. Far from being contradictory, these contexts reinforced the timelessness of Hepworth's project. Her forward-looking sculptures, like the ritualistic stone structures of the past, were intended to serve a communal function by uniting people around the highest social values.

MOVE TO CORNWALL

The outbreak of war in 1939 brought international cooperation between modern artists to a halt. Hepworth and Nicholson, perhaps sensing the inevitability of conflict, had taken their young triplets to stay with the painters Adrian Stokes and Margaret Mellis in Carbis Bay, close to the Cornish harbour town of St Ives in West Penwith. Wishing to keep their children out of harm's way, they remained with their friends for the first four months of the war before finding a house nearby. In September, Gabo arrived in Carbis Bay, his presence giving further structure to a new configuration of abstract artists in Cornwall which also included Peter Lanyon, John Wells and Wilhelmina-Barns Graham.

Despite this promising artistic community, Hepworth's wartime existence in St Ives was challenging: art materials were scarce, and it was not until her family moved to a larger house in Carbis Bay in 1942 that she had the space to carve sculptures again. Moreover, Nicholson frequently returned to London, leaving her to care for the triplets. She wrote to her friend and supporter, the critic E. Hartley Ramsden, of the grinding daily cycle that involved mending, gardening and feeding the children. 'I think the secret lies in not resisting the chores & the drudgery', she explained, '& in carrying the creative mood on with oneself while cooking so that it is unbroken.'[20]

STRINGS & COLOUR

Shortly before leaving London in 1939 Hepworth pioneered an innovative plaster carving, in which she scooped out the centre of the form and used blue paint and red strings to accentuate the tensions between inner and outer space. In Cornwall, hampered by limited time, space and materials, she developed this concept via small maquettes and two-dimensional works that suggested the presence of colour and strings with blocks of gouache and incised pencil lines (pp.52, 53).

Despite having created her initial carving in London, Hepworth consistently associated these formal elements with Cornwall. Looking out over its rocky peaks, lush valleys and encircling coves, she was struck by the immersive atmosphere of this coastal landscape, and directly linked her experience with the steps she was taking in her art. 'The colour in the concavities plunged me into the depth of water, caves, or shadows deeper than the carved concavities themselves. The strings were the tension I felt between myself and the sea, the wind or the hills', she later reflected.[21]

When Hepworth resumed carving in the summer of 1943, she advanced this preoccupation with interior space to a new level. In *Oval Sculpture* 1943 (p.54) she penetrated a log with five piercings, creating a complex pattern of curving contours and cavities which gave the impression of the external structure

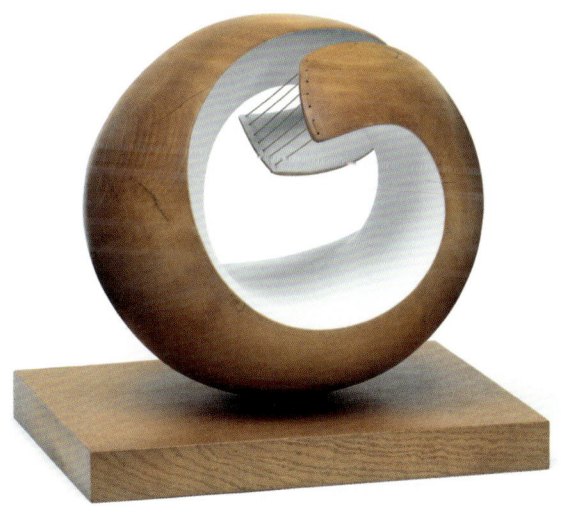

Pelagos 1946
Elm, paint and strings on
oak base
43 × 46 × 38.5

17

enfolding the interior space. Elsewhere she introduced pale blue paint and tight threads. In *Pelagos* 1946 (p.17) strings connect the ends of the sculpture's two inner spirals, echoing the way that Hepworth saw the sides of St Ives Bay as embracing arms.

Ramsden recognised this approach as phenomenological, noting that Hepworth's blend of constructivist components and organic forms created an interconnection between the beholder, the art object and its surroundings. For her, Hepworth's carvings were essentially durational since they existed within the realm of nature and evoked 'a sense of the cosmic rhythm of life' that was ongoing and regenerative.[22]

POSTWAR RECONSTRUCTION

The idea that art could be restorative was particularly powerful in the aftermath of devastating global conflict. The USA and Soviet Union emerged from the ruins of the Second World War as competing superpowers, setting in motion a potentially catastrophic nuclear arms race that compelled mankind to consider its future obliteration. In response to this existential threat the United Nations was established, with the aim of maintaining international peace and security.

Hepworth, still living and working in Cornwall, was acutely aware of these world developments. As an advocate for the Campaign for Nuclear Disarmament and later a member of the British Labour Party, she participated in national discourses surrounding social reconstruction. Meanwhile, from an artistic standpoint, she reflected upon how such far-reaching trauma had altered the utopian project of constructivism. In the wake of events such as the dropping of nuclear bombs on Hiroshima and Nagasaki, Hepworth stated: 'It is hopeless to presume that I, or anybody thinks the same as in 1936, either about Art, Philosophy, or Religion.'[23]

Nevertheless, she continued to view art as a purposeful, vitalising force, describing her sculpture as a 'completely logical way of expressing the intrinsic "will to life" as opposed to the extrinsic disaster of the world war'.[24] Crucially, Hepworth distanced herself from the utilitarian doctrines of Russian constructivism associated with Gabo, who left Cornwall for the US in 1946. Instead she argued for the use of the term 'constructive' to describe art and creative concepts that served broadly as forces for positive change in the world.

THE HOSPITAL DRAWINGS

Just before the end of the war, Hepworth's daughter Sarah suffered from a severe bone infection and was treated at the Princess Elizabeth Orthopaedic Hospital in Exeter. After her recovery, Sarah's consultant, the revered surgeon Norman Capener, maintained a close friendship with the family. This was the era in which the fledgling National Health Service was established in Britain, and Hepworth drew parallels between her own profession and that of the medical practitioners, such as Capener, who she considered key players in rebuilding the nation. Receptive to her ideas, Capener invited her to sketch live surgical operations between 1947 and 1949.

The figurative pictures Hepworth developed from this unique experience are known collectively as the 'hospital drawings' and portray the generalised movements of nurses and consultants working in unity, most frequently the rhythm of the surgeon's hands during operations which the artist identified with her own use of tools and materials. Above all Hepworth was struck by the 'extraordinary beauty of purpose and coordination between human beings dedicated to the saving of life'. During the late 1940s she pursued this interest in human relationships, creating semi-abstract carvings that depicted pairs or groups of figures in varying degrees of communication (pp.62-3). Hepworth noted the ease with which she moved between abstract and figurative modes in her paintings and sculptures, stating: 'The two ways of working flow into each without effort. [They] enhance each other by giving an absolute freedom.'[25]

AN ARTIST IN SOCIETY

In 1951 Hepworth was one of several modern artists invited to make work for the Festival of Britain on London's South Bank. This popular national exhibition was a landmark moment in the nation's postwar recovery, promoting a vision of Britain's future founded on cooperation in science, industrial design, architecture and the arts. Responding to this agenda, Hepworth devised *Contrapuntal Forms* 1950-1 (p.20), the title referencing a musical term describing independent yet harmonious melody lines. The composition itself comprised two semi-abstract vertical figures which were physically separate yet had a strong spatial relationship to one another, thus evoking the possibility of interaction.

Hepworth's second contribution, the kinetic sculpture *Turning Forms* 1950–1 (p.64), was situated outside a futuristic-

Installation view of
Contrapuntal Forms at the
Festival of Britain, 1951

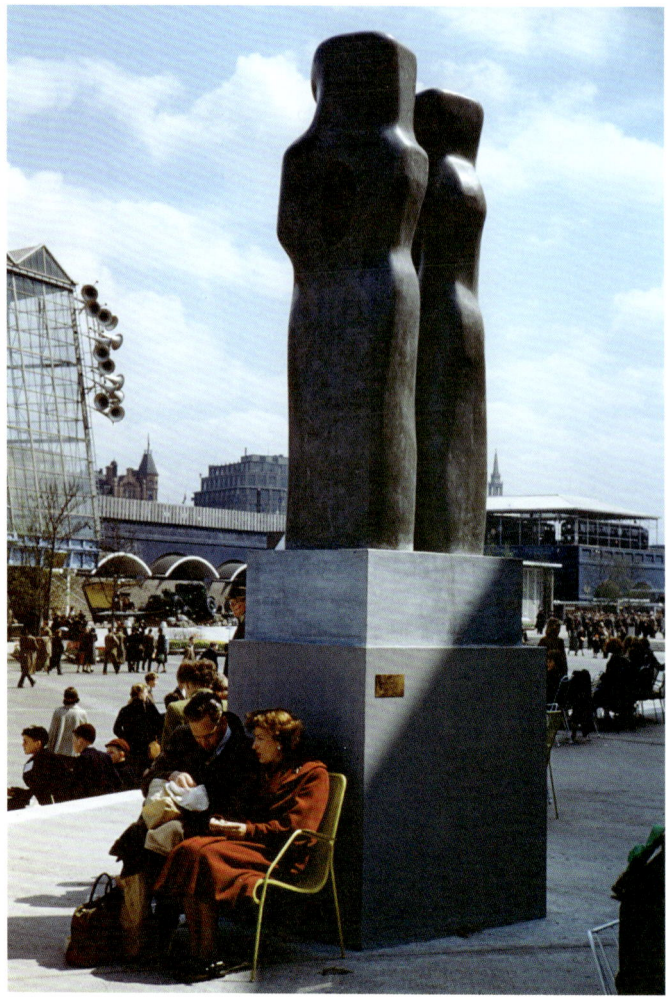

looking restaurant designed by the modernist architect Jane Drew and had at its centre a helix that slowly rotated on a motorised plate. Together, these commissions referenced music, movement and the visual arts alongside themes of social and technological progress, while demonstrating that varying types of abstract sculpture had a place in modern Britain. Following the festival the works were transferred to public sites in Harlow New Town and St Albans in line with postwar initiatives to place 'good' art within emerging suburban communities.

Hepworth's participation in the Festival of Britain was one of several projects that secured her prominent public status after the war. In 1950 she represented Britain at the Venice Biennale, followed in 1954 by a retrospective of her work at the Whitechapel Gallery in London. This momentum was sustained by a major monograph, published in 1952, with a preface by Herbert Read. Nevertheless, Hepworth's path was not without challenges. She complained that sexist attitudes caused her to be sidelined in favour of her male peers, and comparisons with Moore, who had been selected for the Biennale two years before her own show, negatively impacted on her success. It certainly seemed that Hepworth was working in Moore's shadow since she was awarded fewer major exhibitions, commissions and public appointments than him. Added to this, her marriage to Nicholson broke down, and the couple divorced in 1951.

A NEW RHYTHM

A turning point came when Hepworth acquired a new property in the centre of St Ives, which served initially as a studio and then, after December 1950, as her home. Later she commented that finding Trewyn Studio 'was a sort of magic'.[26] Here was space to undertake larger public projects and launch herself as an independent artist. Hepworth hired permanent assistants for the first time, converted outbuildings into workspaces and even redesigned the garden. In this venture she was assisted by a new friend, the South African-born composer Priaulx Rainier, who helped select trees and exotic plants around which Hepworth arranged her sculptures.

It was in Trewyn's garden that Rainier composed the fragment Rhythms of the Stones, inspired by the sound of Hepworth and her assistants carving Contrapuntal Forms. In turn, the artist was motivated by Rainier to give greater prominence to music in her practice, which extended to making sets and costumes for entire productions.

Hepworth contributed to two theatrical projects in London's West End: a restaging of Sophocles's Electra at the Old Vic in 1951 and the presentation of Michael Tippett's opera The Midsummer Marriage at the Royal Opera House in 1955 (p.22). Electra's stage set featured a representation of the god Apollo formed from bent steel rod, Hepworth's first metal sculpture in over three decades (p.65).

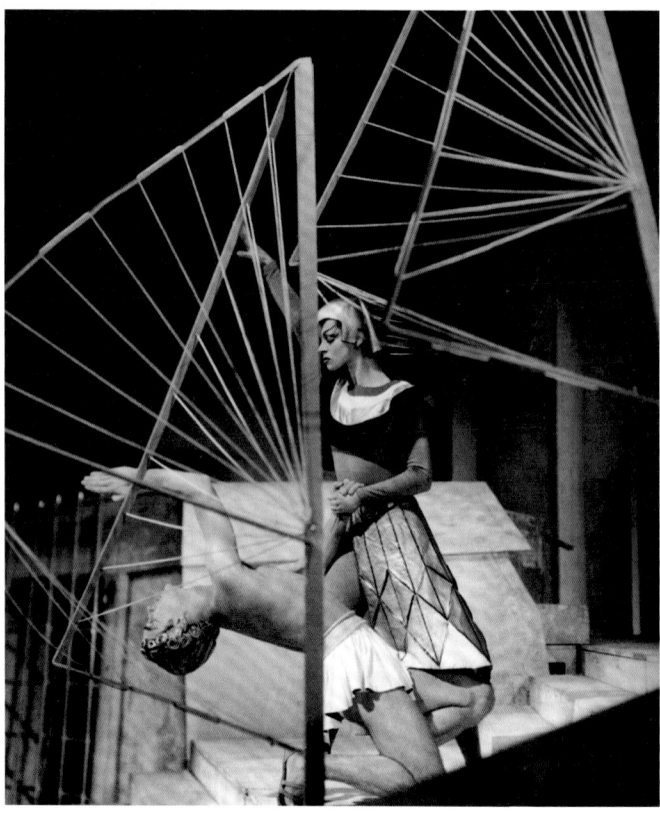

Photograph showing Hepworth's *Ritual Dance Constructions* for *The Midsummer Marriage* 1955

COPING WITH LOSS

In February 1953 Hepworth's elder son Paul was killed in an air crash while on active service with the Royal Air Force in Thailand. Hepworth's close friend and patron Margaret Gardiner later referred to this devastating loss as the artist's lasting grief. Afterwards Hepworth sought comfort and, on some level, acceptance through her work. One figurative carving entitled *Madonna and Child* 1954 (p.67) evoked ideas of collective bereavement through religious symbolism, while the painting *Two Figures (Heroes)* 1954 (p.66) and sculpture *Monolith (Empyrean)* 1953 (opposite) drew inspiration from the German poet Rainer Maria Rilke, whose writings reassured Hepworth during her darkest moments. She carved linked hollows through the head and stomach of *Monolith (Empyrean)*, a device she posited as 'the bridge between the body and the mind seeking comprehension'.[27]

In August 1954, Gardiner invited Hepworth on a cruise

around Greece and its islands, taking in Athens, Mycenae, Delphi, Crete, Rhodes and Santorini. The trip was intended to lift the artist out of her sorrow, at least temporarily, by connecting her with a place that had been a lifelong source of inspiration, although she had never visited before. Standing alone in this ancient, elemental environment, Hepworth was able to philosophise on her own being, as well as death as part of life's cycle.

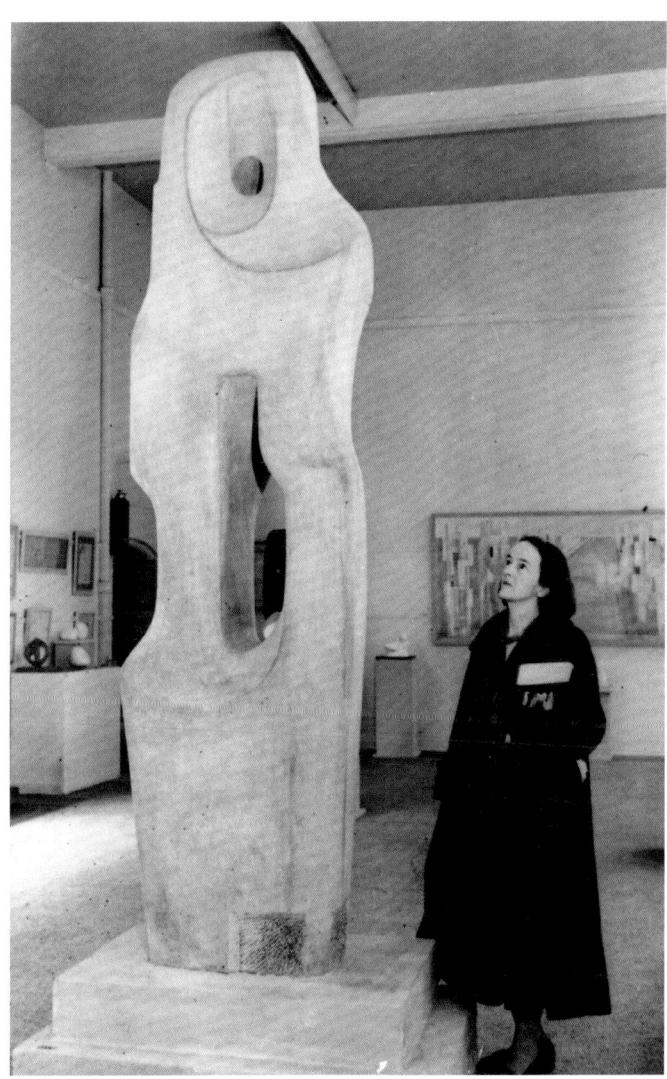

Hepworth alongside
Monolith (Empyrean) at her
Whitechapel exhibition
retrospective in 1954

Delos (The Aegean Suite) 1971
Lithograph on paper
76.7 × 54.5

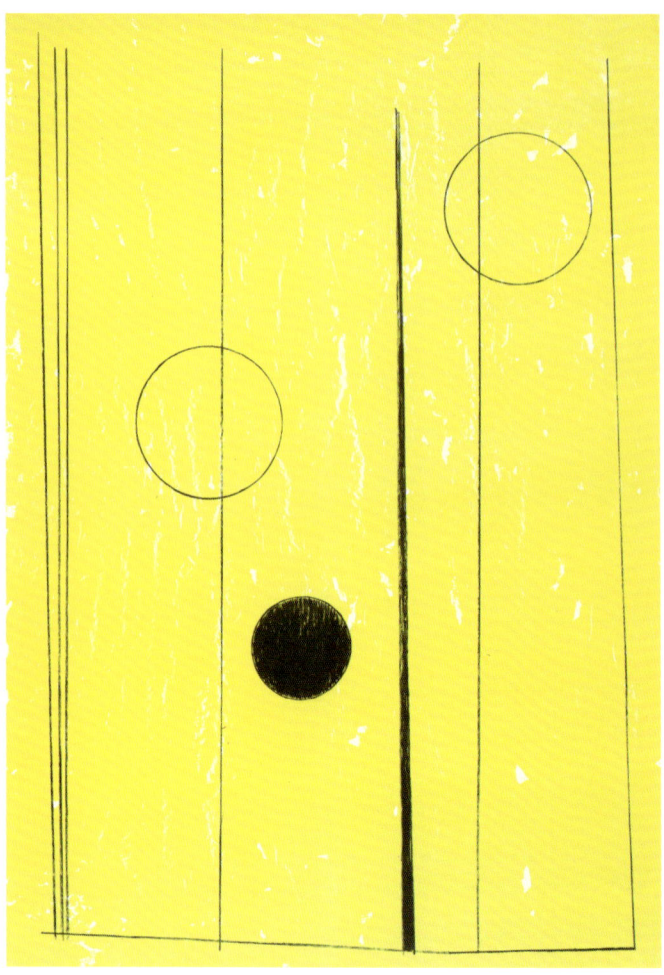

Over the next two decades she reflected upon her Greek
experience in several important works. Immediately after
the Mediterranean tour in 1954–6, and then again between
1960 and 1963, she channelled her emotions into ambitious
carvings cut from gigantic guarea logs, which were sourced
via Gardiner, from Nigeria. Across the two groups seven of the
sculptures had names associated with Greece (pp.68, 69, 71).
Again, Hepworth found solace in her work, comforted by what
she described as the 'most beautiful, hard lovely warm timber'
with its strong cedar aroma.[28] Tunnelling through these
immense structures, she responded to the landscape much as

she had with *Pelagos*: as one continuous, enfolding form. Later, in 1971 she synthesised the Greek trip into a series of lithographs entitled *The Aegean Suite* (opposite, p.89) which distilled her experiences of isolation, pure existence and spiritual ascent.

TURN TO METAL

Five years after her experimental use of steel rods in *Apollo*, Hepworth began to rigorously explore metal as a medium for her sculpture. In part, this step was influenced by younger sculptors such as Reg Butler and Kenneth Armitage, labelled 'geometry of fear' artists by Read because they expressed postwar anxieties through skeletal forms made in bronze, iron and copper. Hepworth, however, only committed to metal when she found it could be used to advance her own aesthetic interests while retaining the same tactile pleasure she derived from carving.

In some cases, Hepworth built on the progress achieved in her theatre designs. She employed brass and copper sheets that could be bent into shape, allowing her to compose dynamic, open forms which echoed her ongoing interest in rhythm and movement. In some sculptures she introduced taut threads that appeared to hold this flexible material in a state of tension (p.73).

Additionally, Hepworth created maquettes to be cast in bronze via an external foundry. In these preparatory prototypes, her approach differed significantly from the clay modelling method she had initially adopted at the beginning of her career. Now she added plaster to a malleable framework of aluminium mesh, before cutting back the form with carving tools once the materials had hardened. The benefits of her technique can be seen in works such as *Curved Form (Trevalgan)* 1956 (p.77) and *Oval Form (Trezion)* 1961–3 (p.26): these bronzes form versatile, swooping lines in space, which were attained by constructing free-standing curved armatures quickly without the need for additional structural reinforcement. Crucially Hepworth always created her maquettes to the same scale as the final bronze casts, the surfaces of which retained all of the markings she had made during the carving process. Hepworth later summarised her approach when she explained, 'I only learned to love bronze when I found that it was gentle and I could file it and carve it and chisel it.'

Hepworth's developments in metal were profoundly

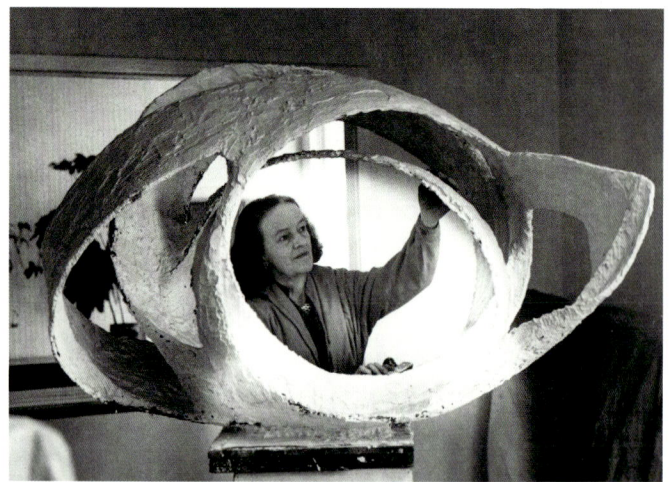

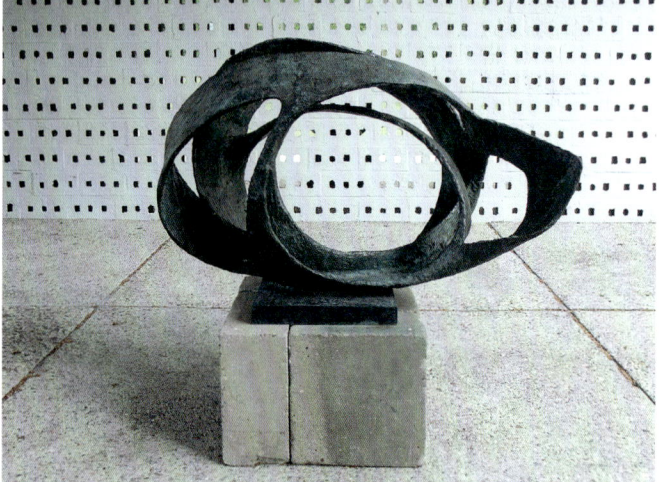

enhanced by her renewed interest in painting. This was driven
by global trends in gestural abstraction, particularly the
Parisian movement tachisme (the name derived from the word
tache, meaning stain or splash), which became associated with
expressive freedom in art and society after the war. Hepworth
cited the spontaneous mark-making of Pierre Soulages as an
influence on her own lyrical, calligraphic style (p.75).[29] The
limitless feeling she evoked in her compositions transferred to
her sculptures, which contained the same linearity, expressive
surface texture and sense of movement.

In addition to its material advantages, metal provided significant professional benefits for Hepworth. By collaborating with foundries to cast her sculptures in editions she was able to produce multiple versions of a single work, sometimes with varying patinas and finishes, which could be sold to different collections and exhibited simultaneously in various display contexts. The robustness of bronze also meant that her casts could better withstand touring schedules, which became more demanding after Hepworth signed commercial contracts with the dealerships Gimpel Fils and Marlborough Fine Art. From the mid-to-late 1950s onwards, her work was seen across Europe, the Americas and Asia in a string of exhibitions, including a major South American tour following her representation at the São Paulo Biennial in 1959.

MONUMENTAL SCULPTURE

Thanks to Hepworth's interest in metal, by the early 1960s her practice had opened up in terms of form, scale and public exposure. One logical progression was to make civic commissions in this medium. In short succession she completed *Meridian* 1958–60 for State House in High Holborn, London (p.80), *Winged Figure* 1961–3 for the exterior of the John Lewis department store on London's Oxford Street (p.81) and *Single Form* 1961–4 for the UN Headquarters in New York (pp.28, 82). When producing these monumental sculptures Hepworth again resisted the traditional method of creating small models and enlarging them via the casting process, but instead built up actual-size prototypes from immense armatures, first in a rented space in St Ives, and then in her second studio, a former dance hall located opposite Trewyn, which she acquired in 1961.

Hepworth's technical ambition was matched by her far-reaching social aspirations. *Single Form* was dedicated to the former Secretary-General of the UN, the late Dag Hammarskjöld, a close friend who she met when he gave a speech in London about global nuclear disarmament. Hammarskjöld, who acquired a carving from Hepworth's 1930s *Single Form* series, shared her belief in the social responsibility of the artist, noting a 'kinship' with his own duty towards international peacekeeping.[30] Hepworth was already planning a sculpture for the UN when Hammarskjöld died in a plane crash in 1961, and a memorial was commissioned instead. Hepworth flattened out her iconic *Single Form* motif so that

Barbara Hepworth
speaking at the unveiling
of the United Nations *Single
Form*, New York, June 1964

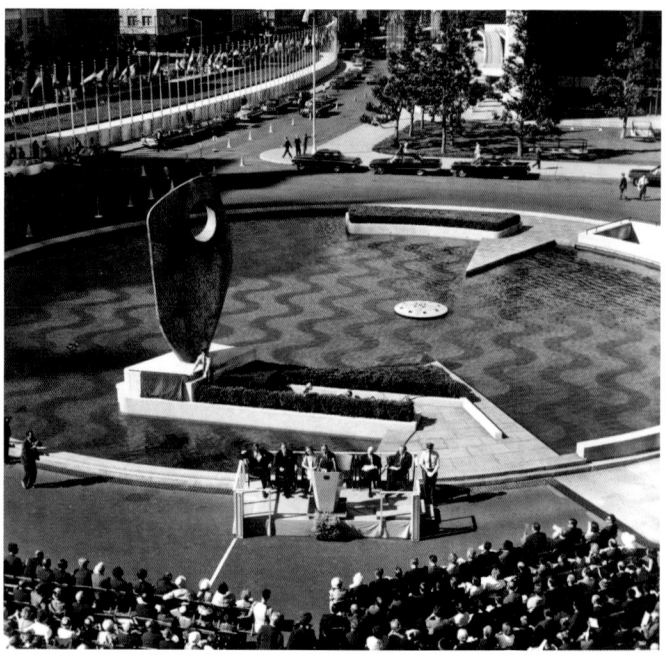

it resembled an irregular shield. The shape embodied
Hammarskjöld's ideological courage, as well as their common
hope for a world shaped by social harmony.

Hepworth was diagnosed with cancer in 1965. Although
she was treated successfully, two years later she broke her hip
and, increasingly immobile, grew ever more reliant on studio
assistants to execute her ideas. Nevertheless, the monumental
sculptures she conceived in the last decade of her life were
among her most ambitious and visionary. The advent of
participatory installation art encouraged her to create *Four-
Square (Walk Through)* 1966 (p.84), into which viewers could
climb. She also pursued her fascination with aviation, which
had broadened from her initial interest in spiritual ascent
to reflect technological advances associated with the
space race. The meditative, grid-like sculpture *Construction
(Crucifixion)* 1966 (opposite) combined religious iconography
with coloured circles suggesting a dynamic planetary orbit.

This contemplative mood continued into the 1970s. Two
immersive, multi-part bronzes, *Conversation with Magic Stones*
1973 (p.85) and *The Family of Man* 1970 (pp.86–7), situated
the viewer within the limitless bounds of time and space,

not so much in relation to an infinite cosmic universe, but instead to an ancient history inspired by rock formations and Neolithic monuments in West Cornwall. In *Conversation with Magic Stones*, figures reminiscent of standing stones were placed in dialogue with three irregular polyhedrons, the eponymous sacred objects, which have alchemical symbolism. For decades Hepworth had explored how her sculptures might facilitate universal understanding between people and their surroundings. Now her spiritual concerns came to the fore, as she considered whether enlightenment might be achieved by connecting to a higher cosmos or plane of existence.

In May 1975 Hepworth died in a fire at her home studio in St Ives, where she had lived and worked for twenty-five years. The following April, Alan Bowness, Hepworth's son-in-law and a future director of Tate, opened Trewyn to the public. Designed to demonstrate her practice and creative development, the Barbara Hepworth Museum fulfilled the artist's desire to shape her legacy. Bowness followed Hepworth's suggestion, expressed in papers to her Trustees

FALLEN IMAGES & NEW NARRATIVES

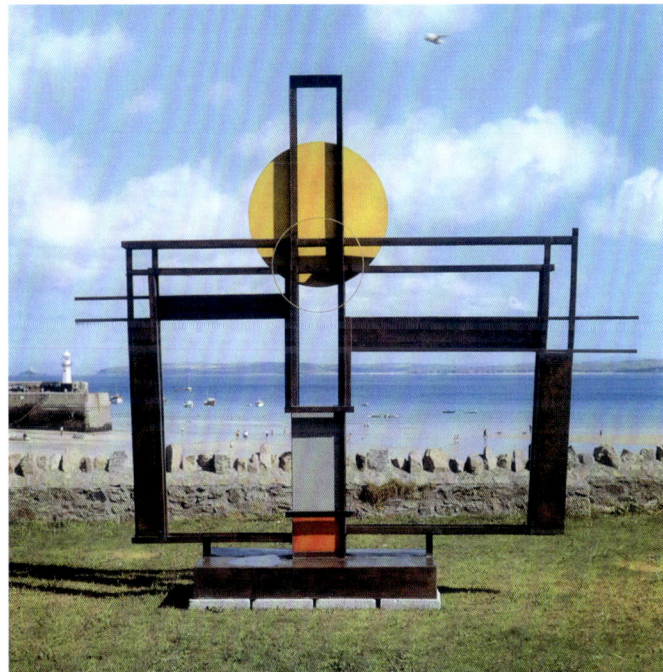

Construction (Crucifixion) 1966-7 in the grounds of St Ia church, next to St Ives harbour
Bronze
390 × 470 × 29

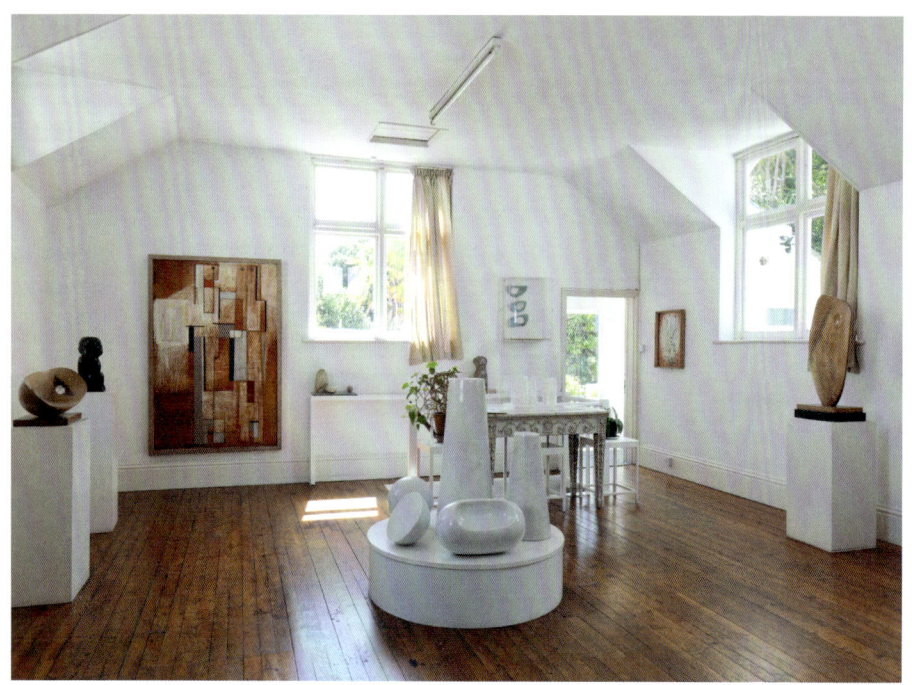

in 1972, that smaller sculptures and paintings be shown on the top floor of her studio and large metal works in the garden; the outdoor workshops were arranged more or less as they had been when she died, so that visitors would have the impression of her work in progress.

Included in the upper-floor display at Trewyn is one of Hepworth's final sculptures, a marble carving entitled *Fallen Images* 1974–5 (above), which had been packed in her studio in preparation for an overseas exhibition at the time of her death. The theme and material invite conflicting interpretations: while Hepworth's use of white marble seems to confirm her persistent belief in the utopian potential of formal purity, the idea of 'fallen images' – implied by elements that appear to have tumbled earthwards – infers instability and even disenchantment. This ambiguity is further confounded by Hepworth's own cryptic explanation made just before she died, in which she stated that the sculpture was 'about images floating in space.'[31]

That we cannot be sure of the meaning of *Fallen Images* highlights the emphatic open-endedness of Hepworth's story,

Installation view of
Fallen Images 1974–5 in
the Barbara Hepworth
Museum, St Ives

despite the narratives formulated in the aftermath of her death. Alongside the Barbara Hepworth Museum – which arguably creates a 'closed', localised impression of her art and studio practice – art historians were quick to locate her career within a narrow modernist lineage in Britain dominated by male artists and critics. It has been the job of Hepworth specialists over the past decades to elaborate a wider history, giving new precedence to aspects sidelined by previous interpretations. One aim has been to overcome the idea that Hepworth was an isolated, 'exceptional' figure among a small handful of influential men, namely Skeaping, Nicholson and Read.[32] As such, a significant number of the professional contacts mentioned in this book have been women, including those working in the fields of art publishing, criticism, curation, music and architecture. Furthermore, it has become clear that in forging a commercially viable practice, Hepworth transgressed normative gendered power dynamics, securing patronage from a mixed group of men and women and setting up studios that employed junior, almost exclusively male, assistants. Meanwhile, Hepworth found equal footing alongside a similarly diverse set of people through her engagement with geopolitical issues. Her affiliations with composers, scientists, diplomats and medical practitioners reveal new national and global contexts.

Rather than merely outlining Hepworth's difficult position within a male-dominated sphere in British art, what we now have is a rich relational orbit in which to situate her art. Her sculptures were remarkable for their extraordinary clarity of vision – her capacity, as Hepworth herself put it, to make concrete a 'beautiful thought.'[33] Nevertheless, wide-reaching philosophies, ideologies and aspirations stood behind her refined concepts and forms. Today we are better placed to recognise this deeply complex, idiosyncratic belief system. To do so is to better understand Hepworth and the ongoing contribution that her art can make to our shared society.

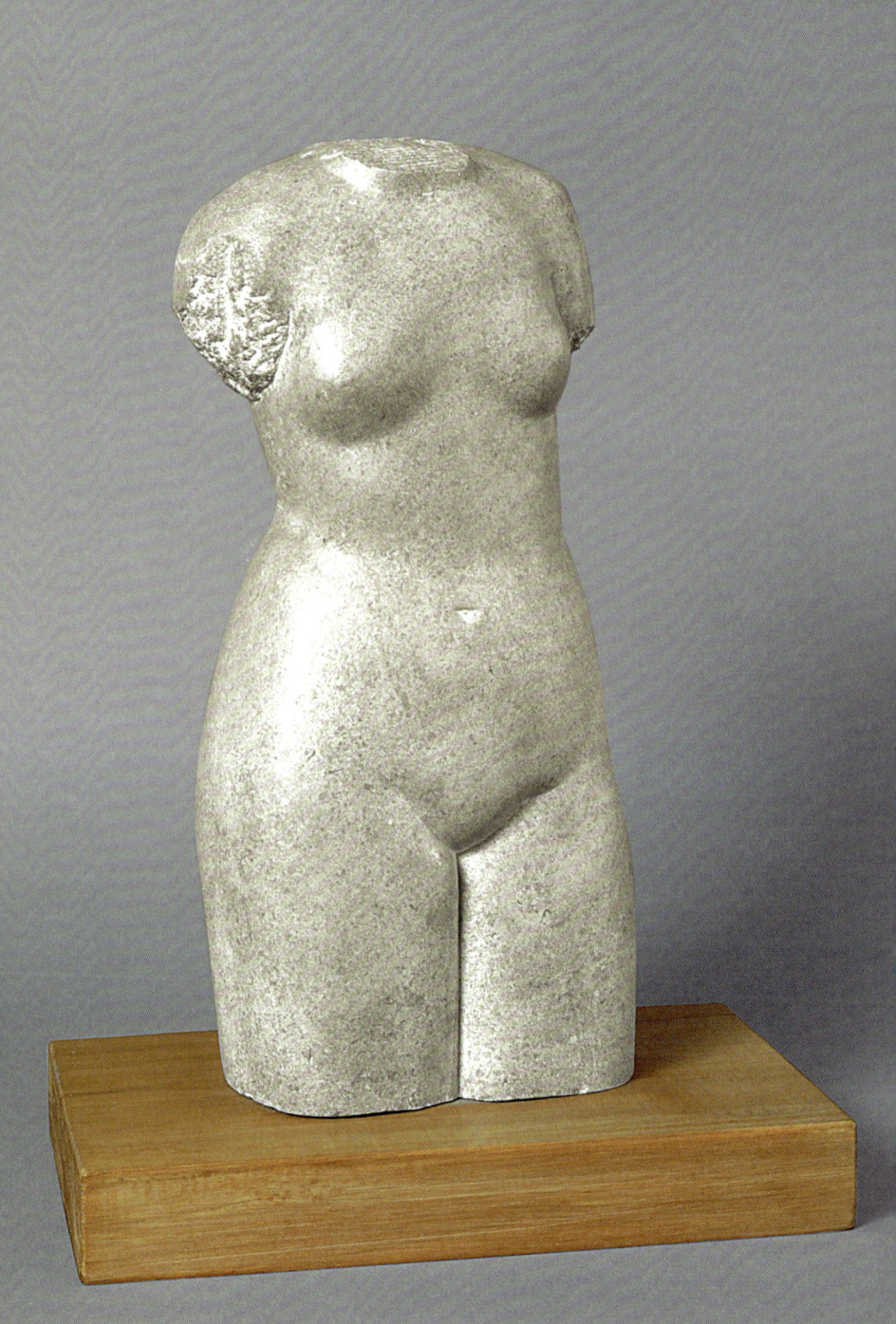

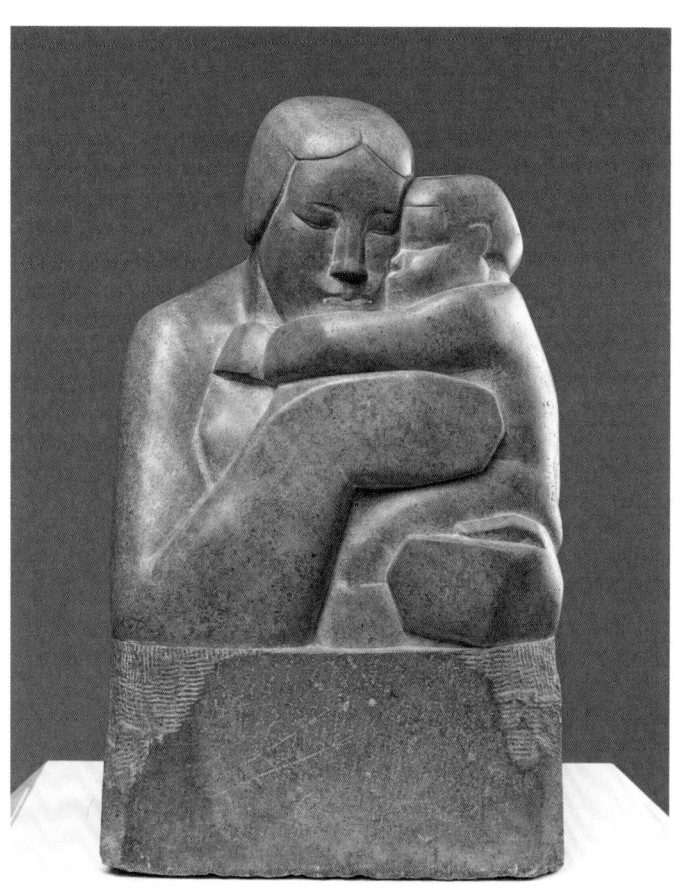

Torso 1928
Hopton Wood stone on
wooden base
36.2 × 17.1 × 10.2

Mother and Child 1927
Hopton Wood stone
45 × 27.6 × 21

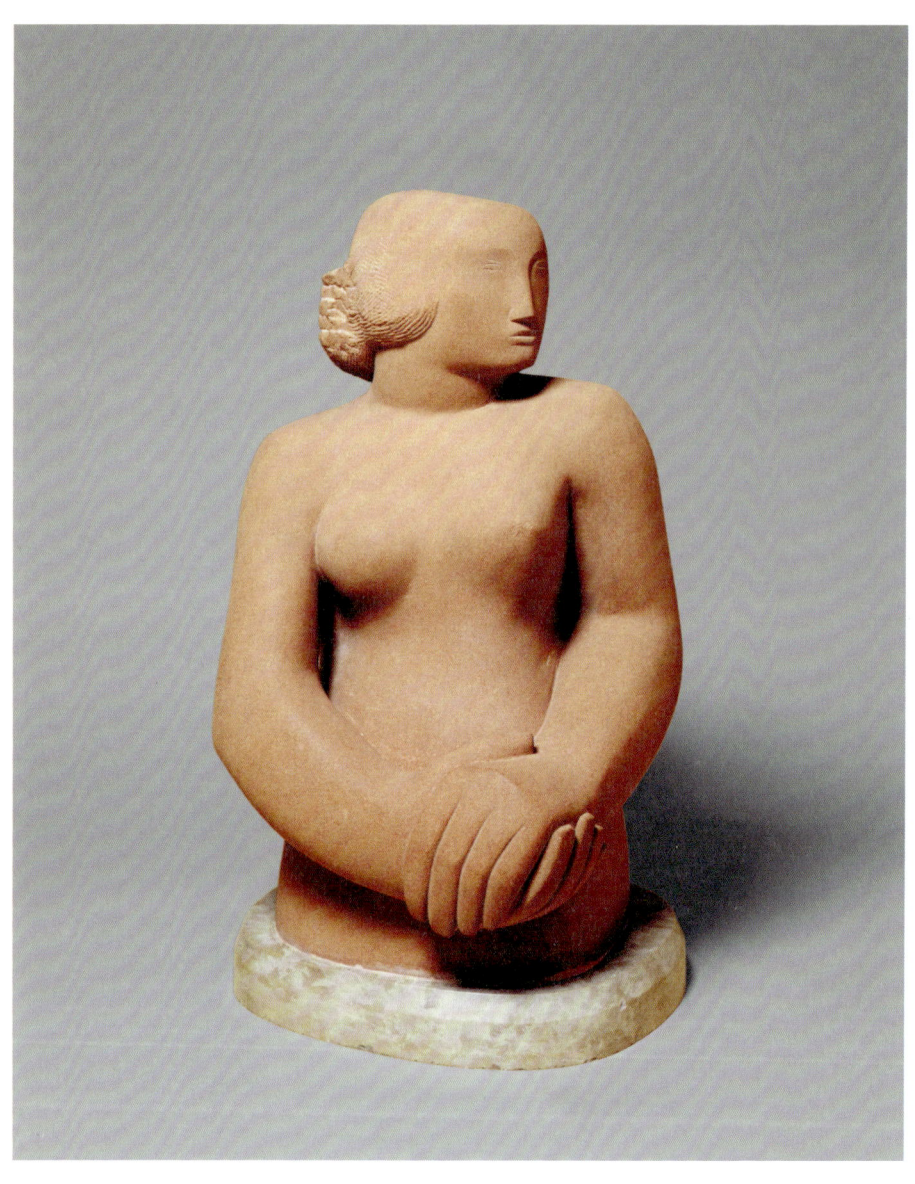

Figure of a Woman 1929–30
Corsehill stone
53.3 x 30.5 x 27.9

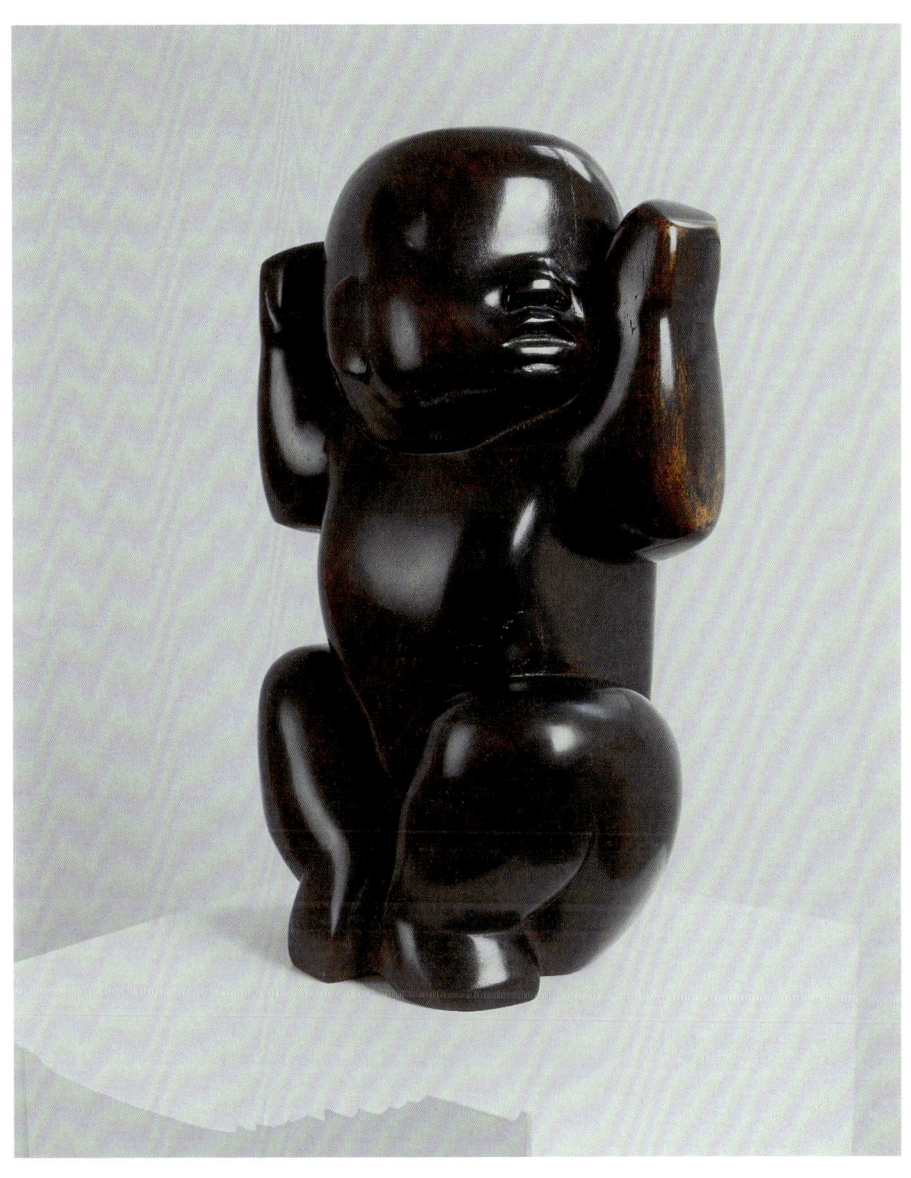

Infant 1929
Burmese wood
43.8 × 27.3 × 25.4

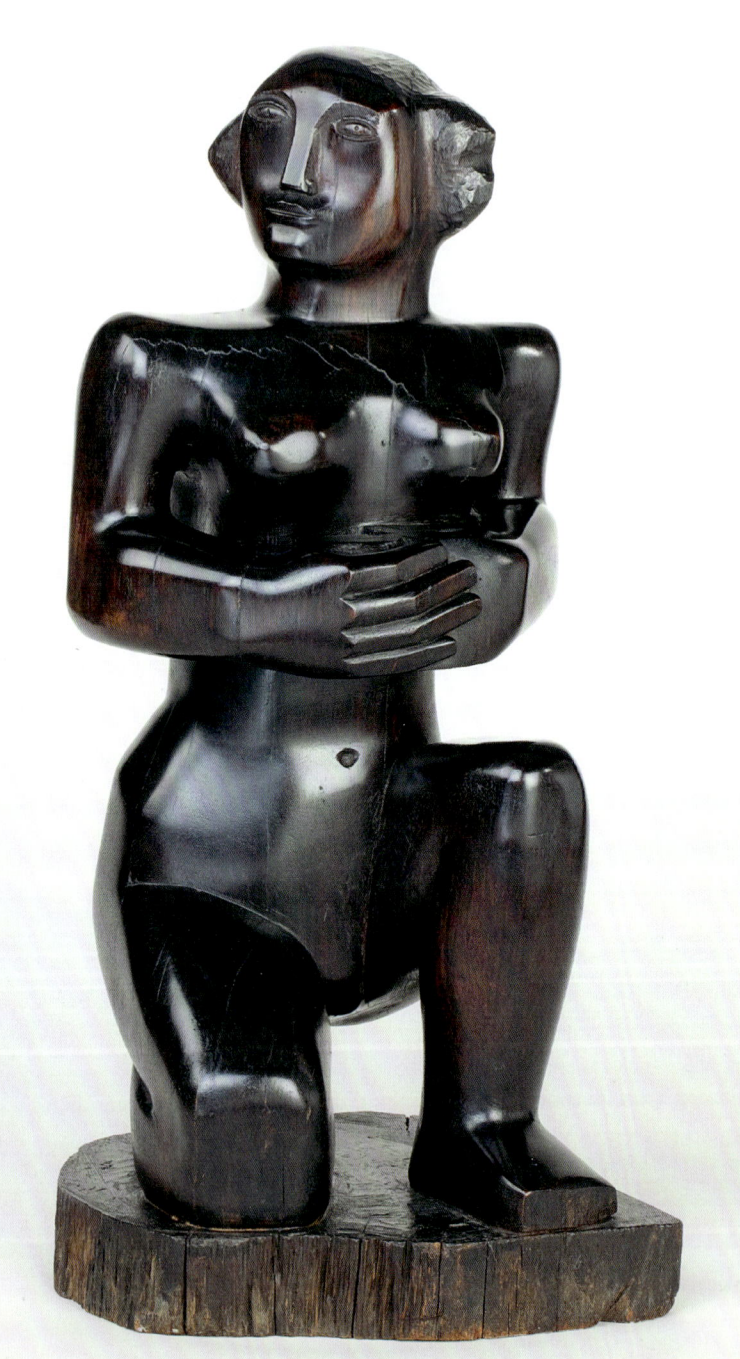

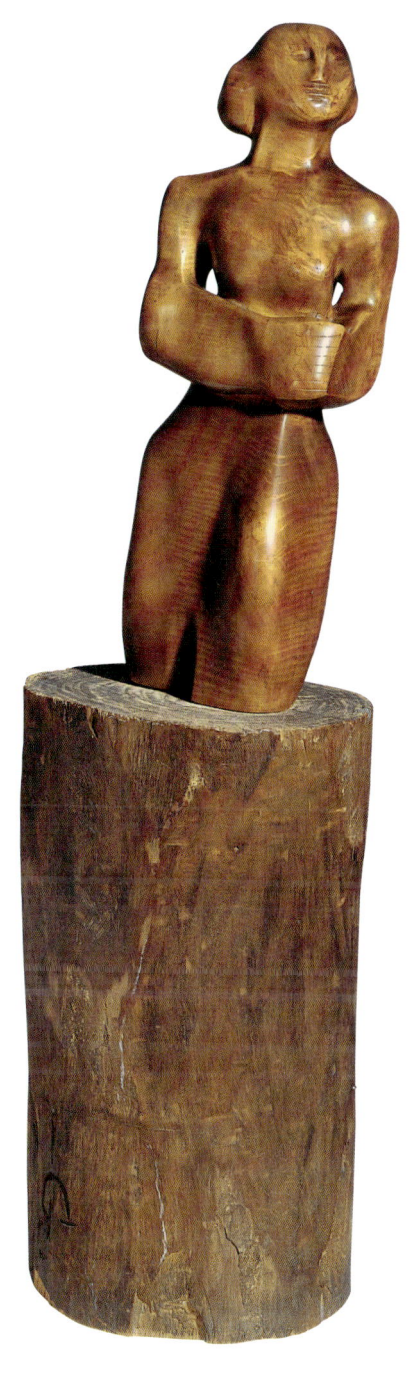

Kneeling Figure 1932
Rosewood
67.5 × 28.8 × 32

Figure in Sycamore 1931
Sycamore
118 × 33 × 33

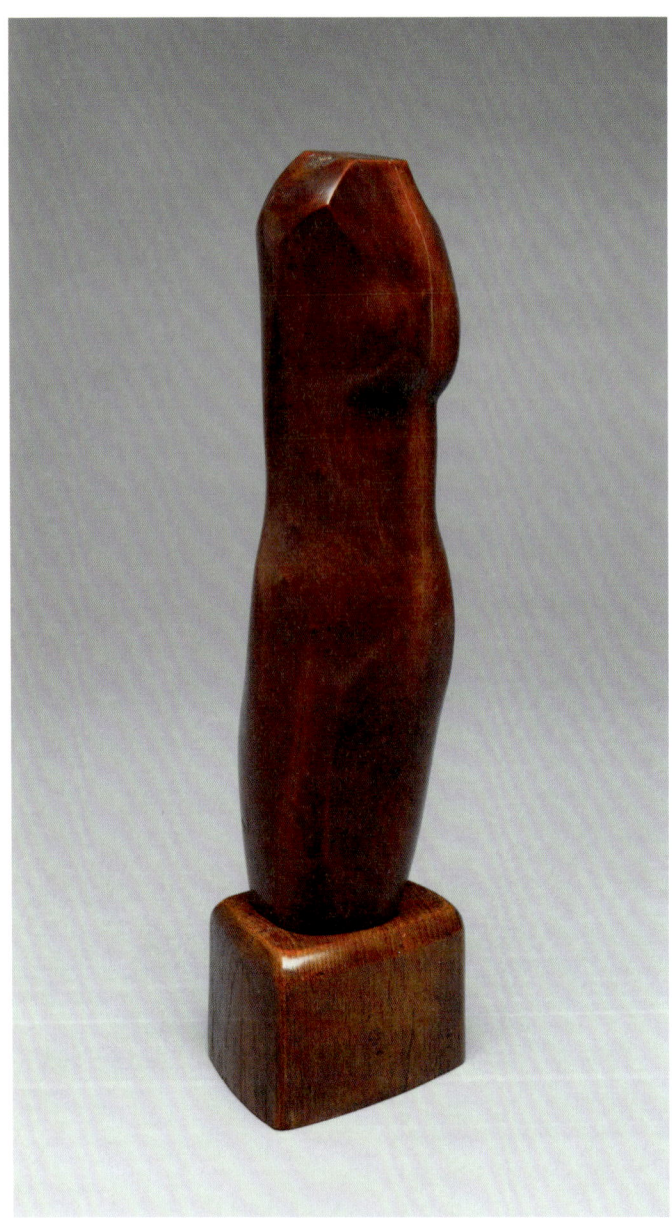

Torso 1929
African ivory wood
33.5 x 9 x 9 (excl. base)

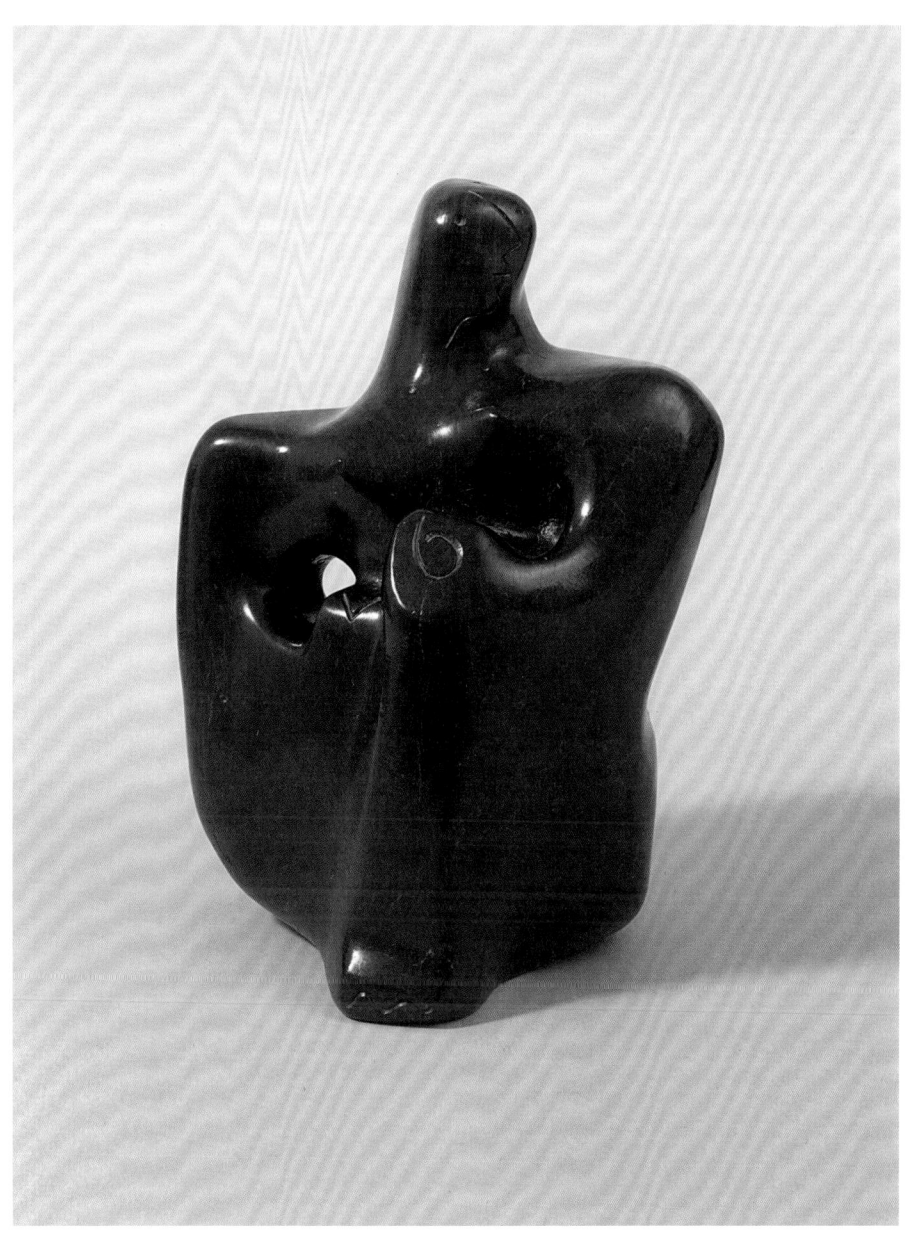

Seated Figure 1932–3
Lignum vitae
35.6 × 26.7 × 21.6

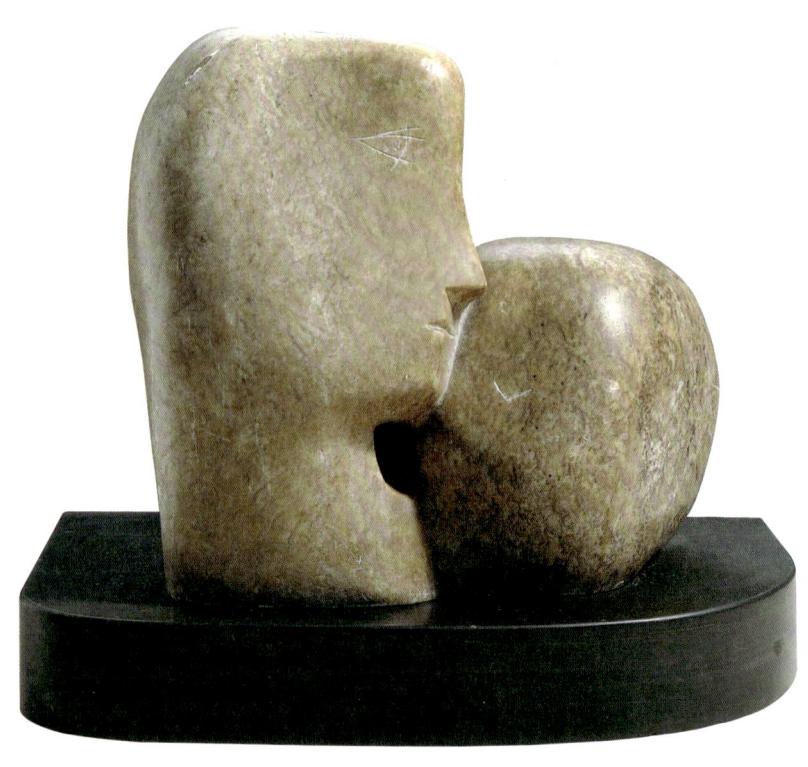

Two Heads 1932
Cumberland alabaster
30 × 38 × 34

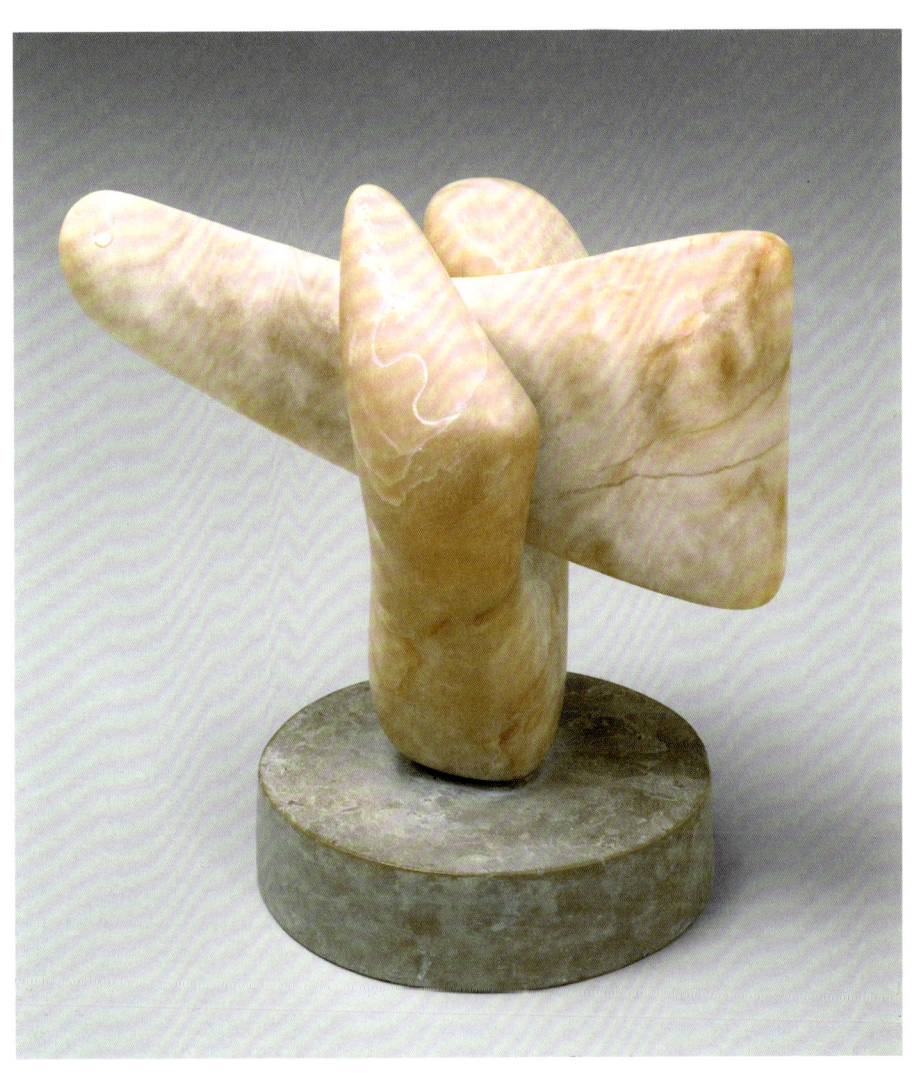

Two Forms 1933
Alabaster on limestone base
26 × 29.6 × 17.6

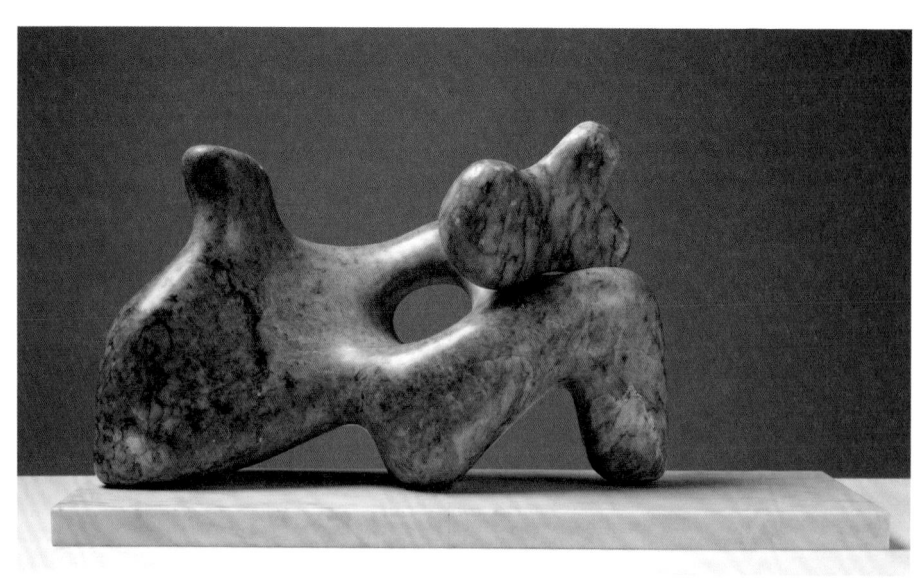

Mother and Child 1934
Cumberland alabaster on
marble base
23 × 45.5 × 18.9

Mother and Child 1934
Pink Ancaster stone
31 × 22 × 26

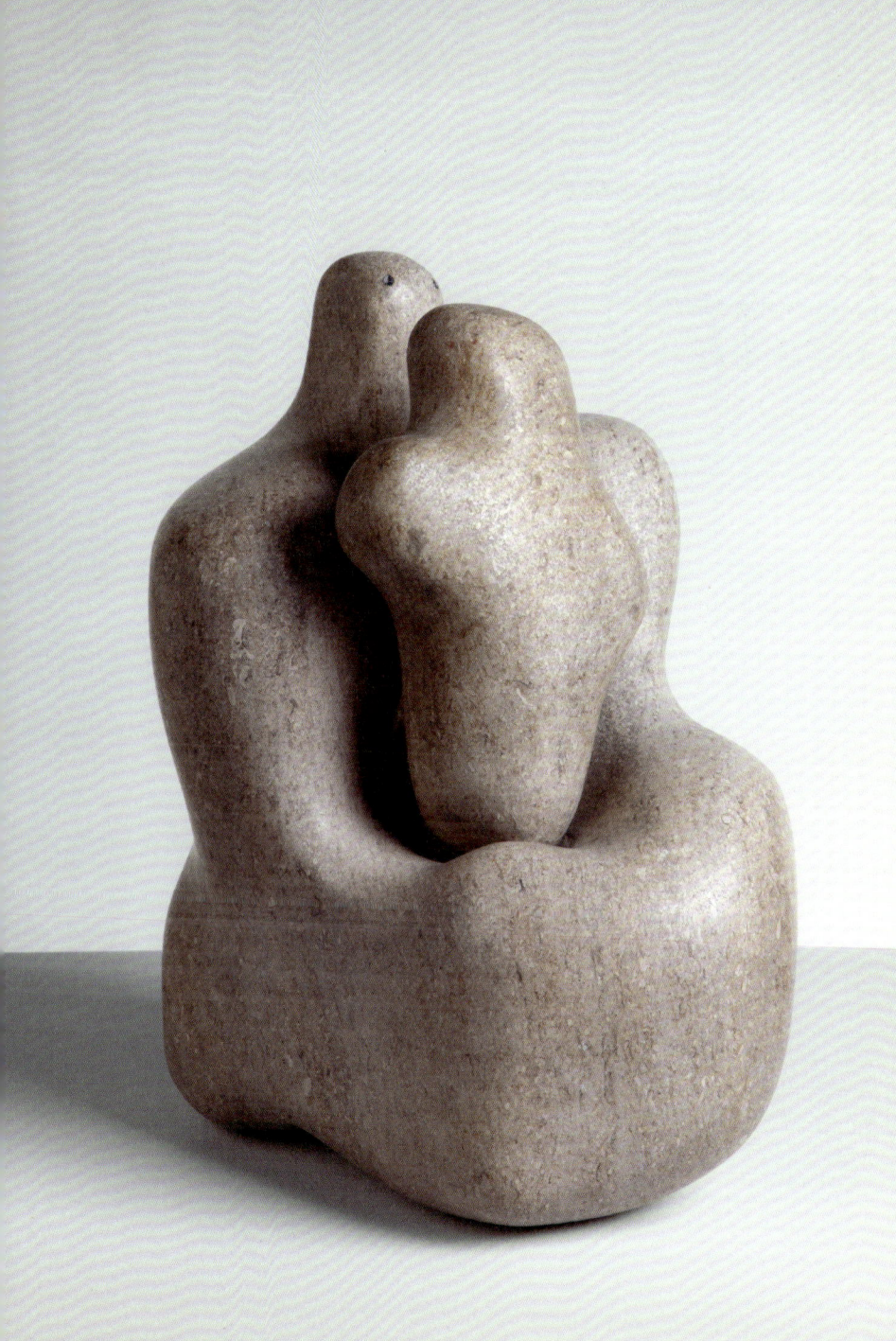

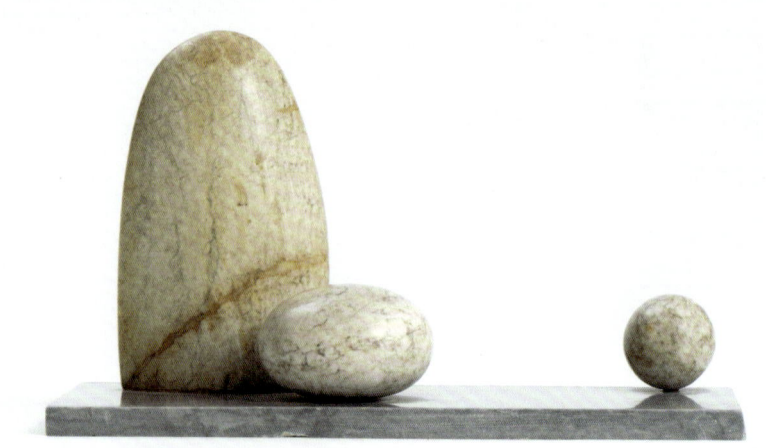

Three Forms (Carving in Grey Alabaster) 1935
Alabaster on marble base
26.5 × 47.3 × 21.7

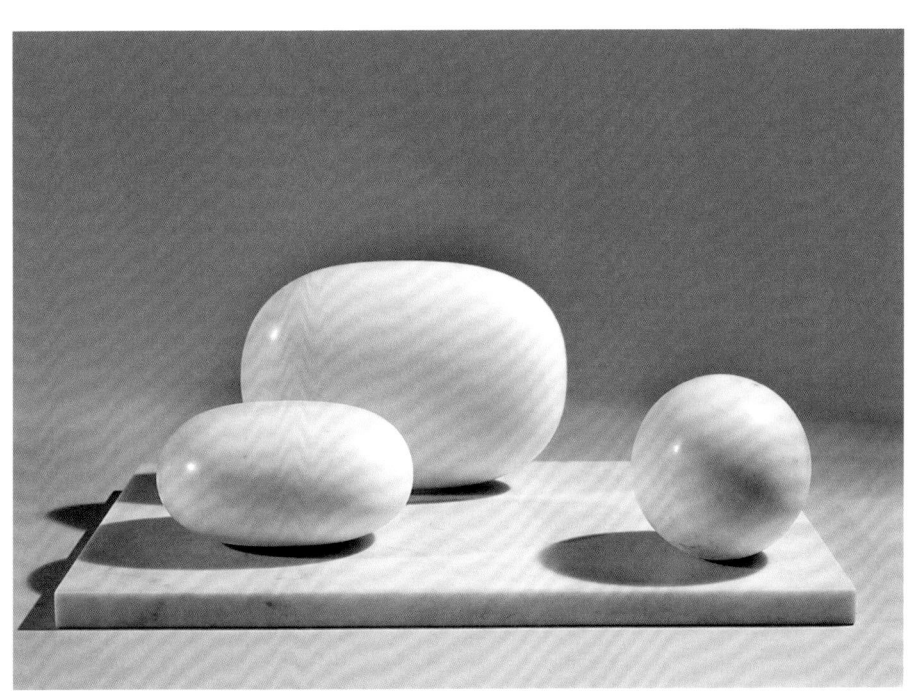

Three Forms 1935
Seravezza marble on
marble base
21 x 53.2 x 34.3

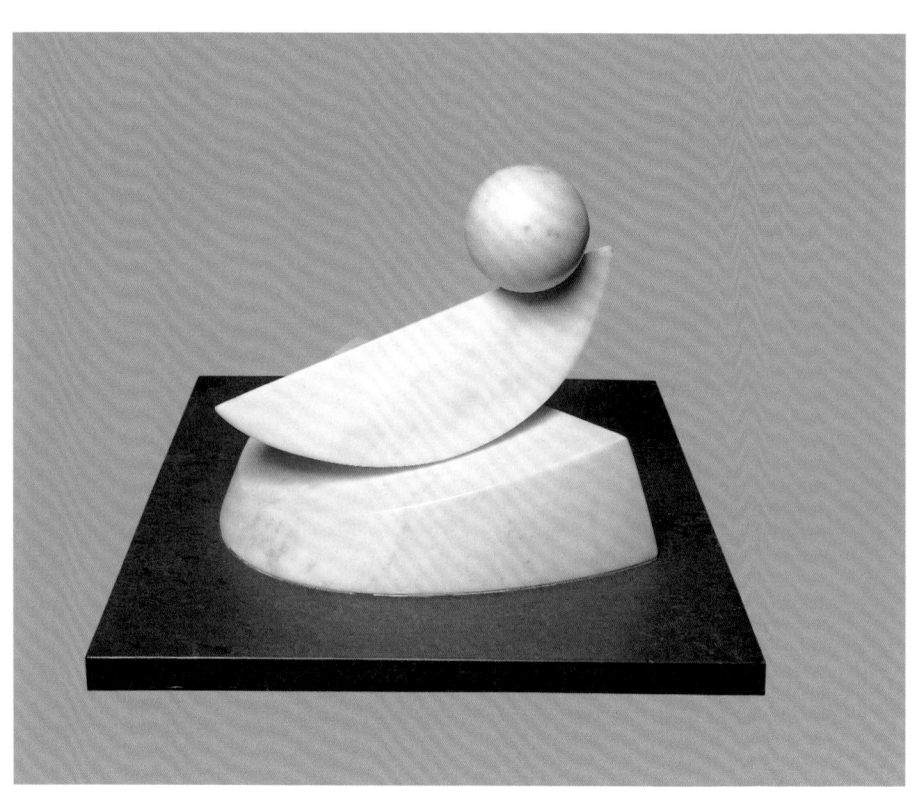

Two Segments and Sphere
1935– 6
White marble
29 × 36 × 37.5

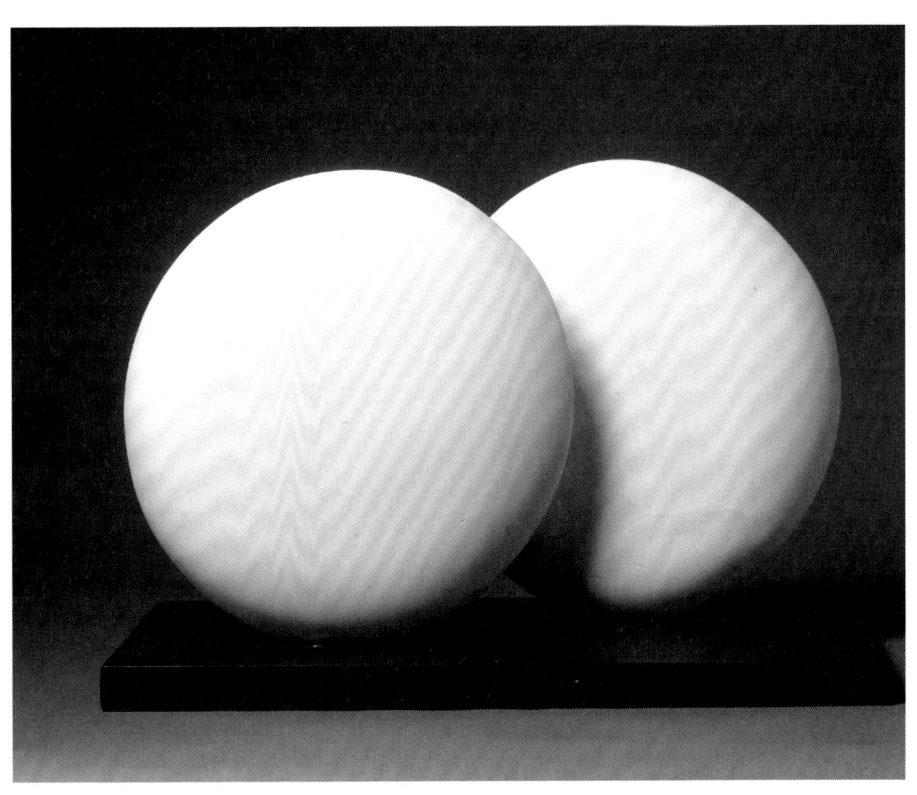

Discs in Echelon, version 2
1935–6
Plaster
35 × 52 × 28

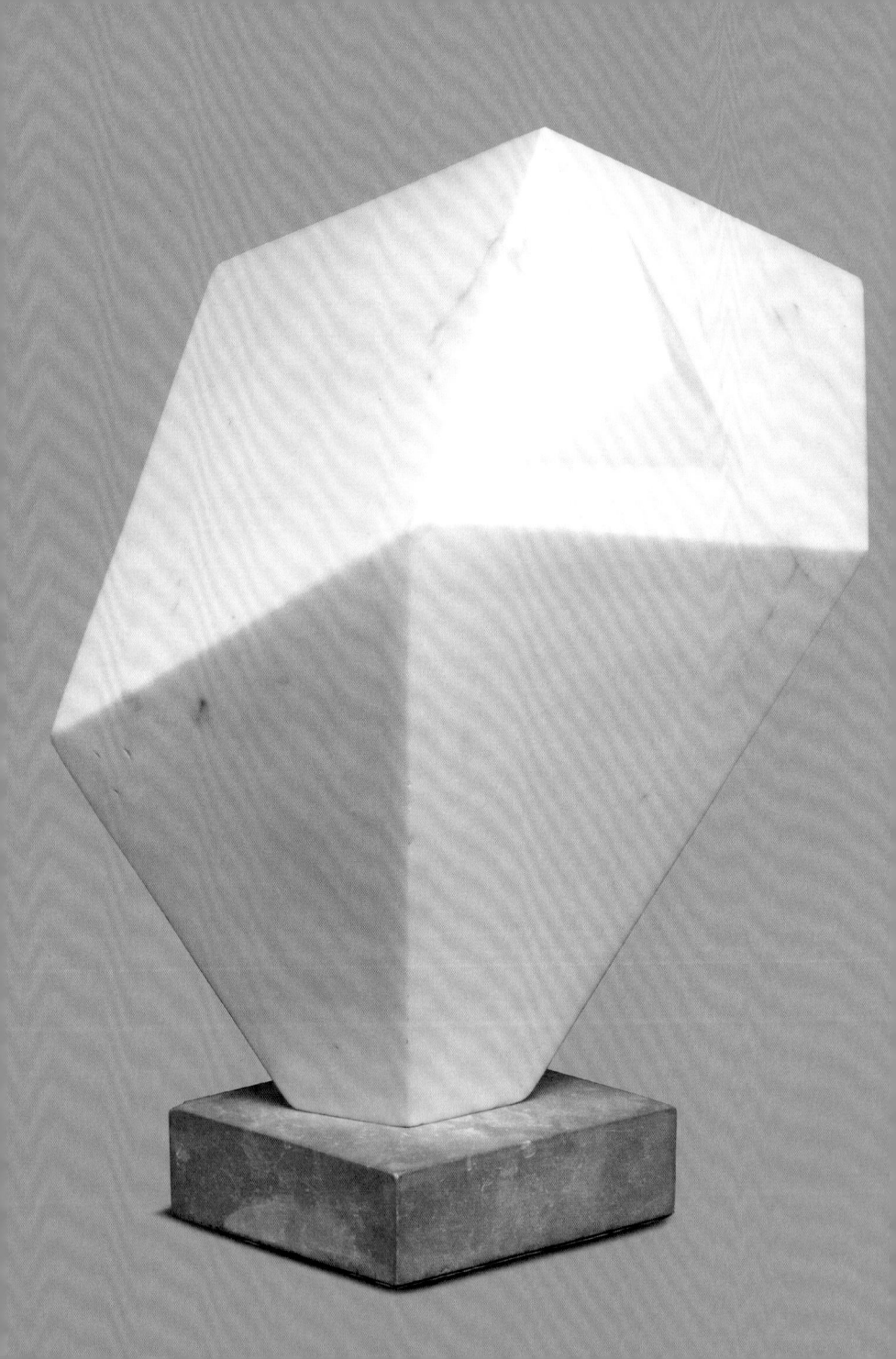

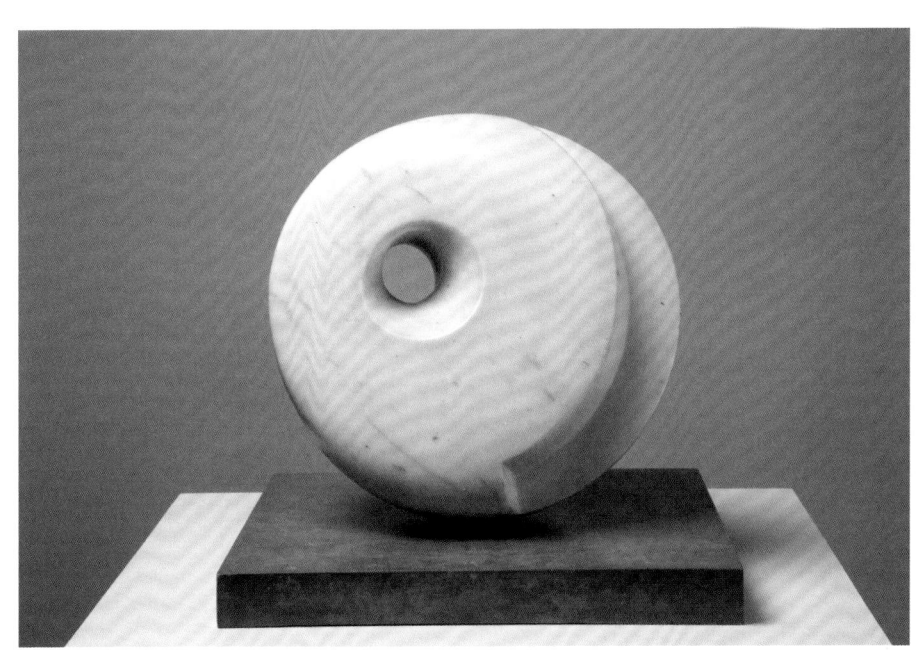

Form 1936
White marble
33 × 22.9 × 37. 5 (excl. base)

Pierced Hemisphere I 1937
White marble
35 × 38 × 38

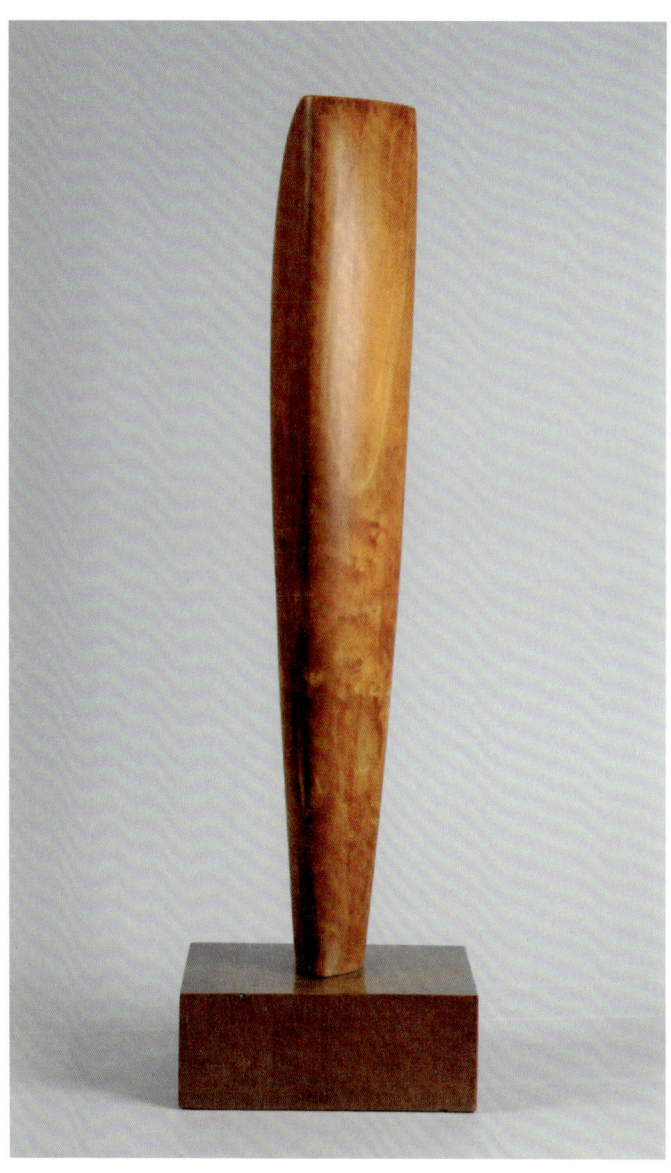

Single Form 1937
Holly wood
122 high (excl. base)

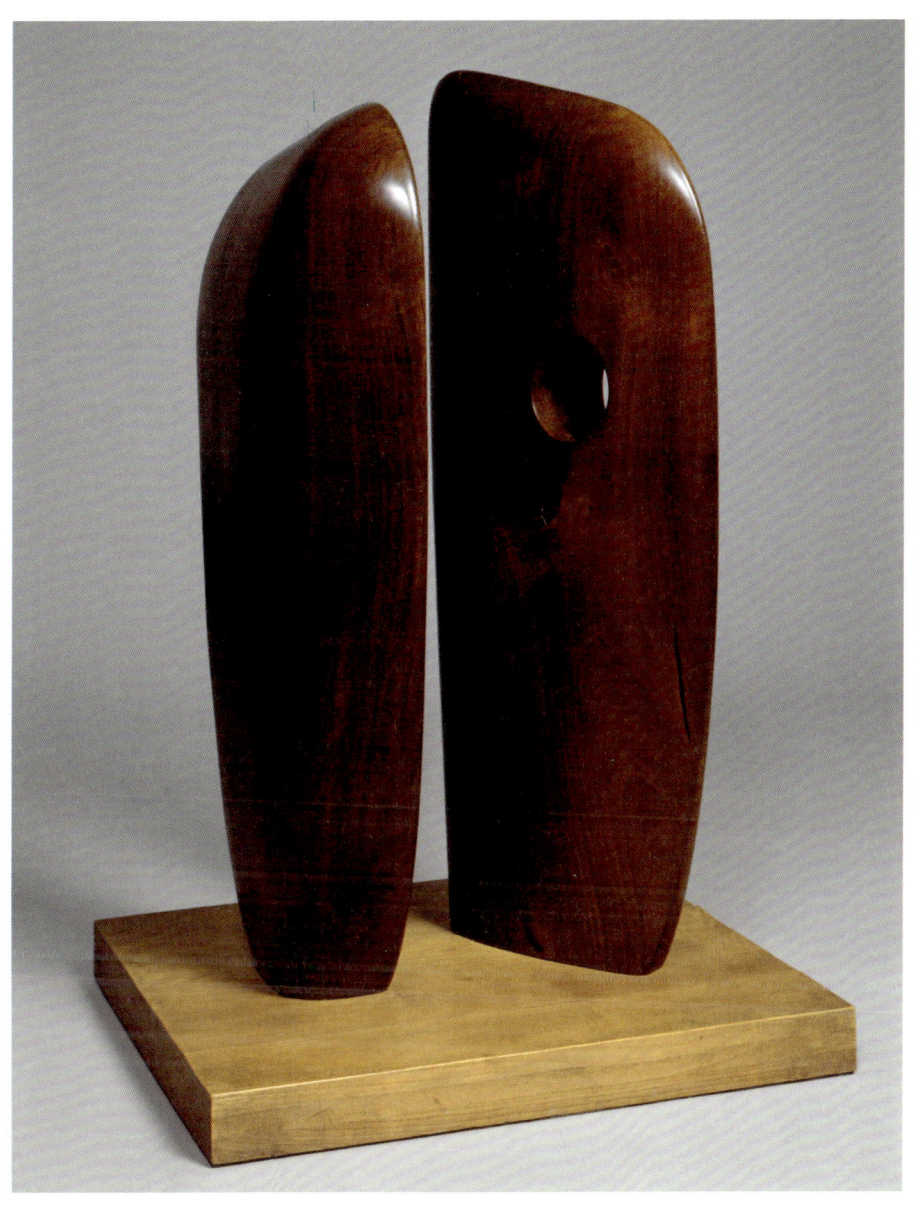

Forms in Echelon 1938
Tulipwood on elm base
108 x 60 x 71

Drawing for 'Sculpture with Colour'
(Forms with Colour) 1941
Gouache, oil paint and graphite
on paper
21.7 × 39.2

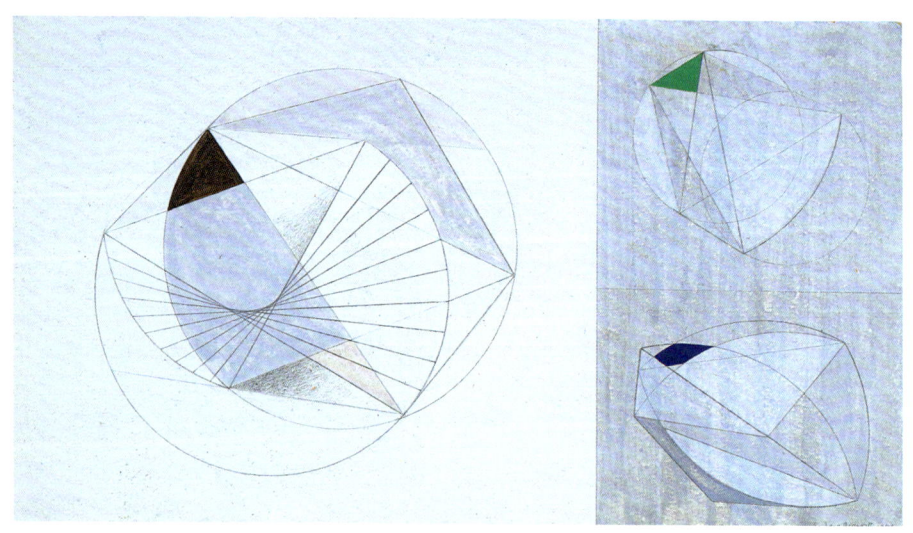

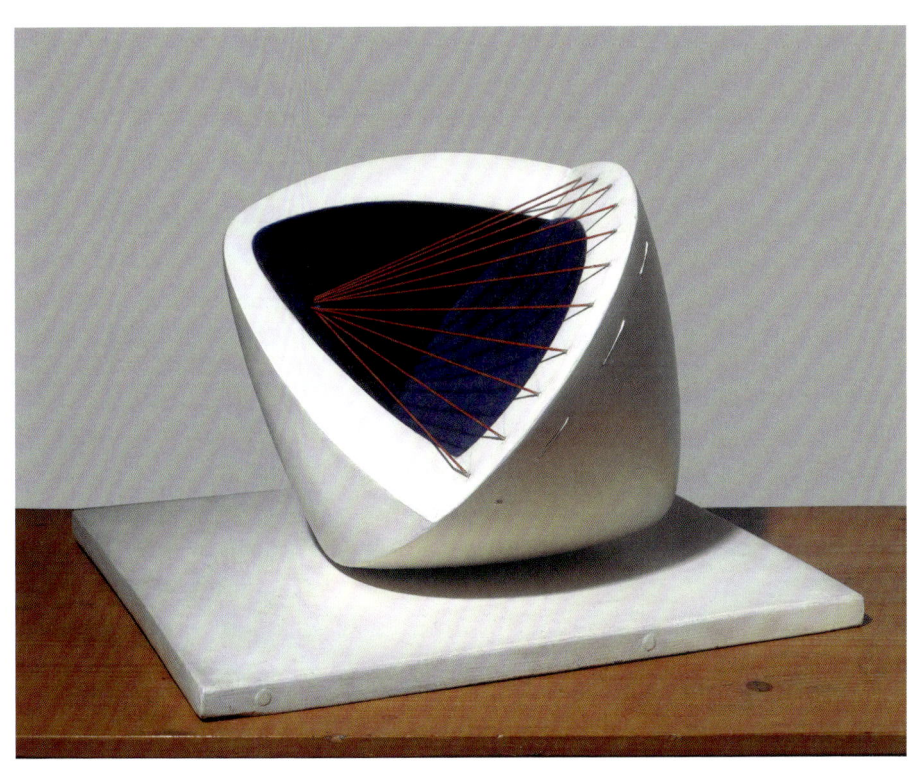

Sculpture with Colour
(Deep Blue and Red) 1943
Wood, paint and strings
25 x 32 x 30 (excl. base)

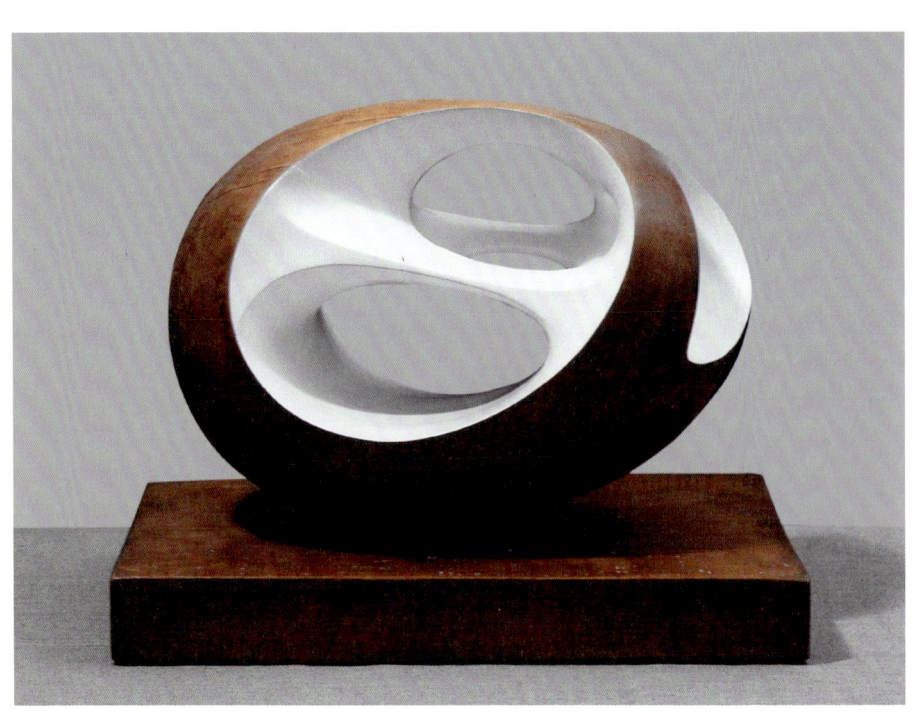

Oval Sculpture 1943
Plane wood and paint
34.9 × 46.2 × 29.9

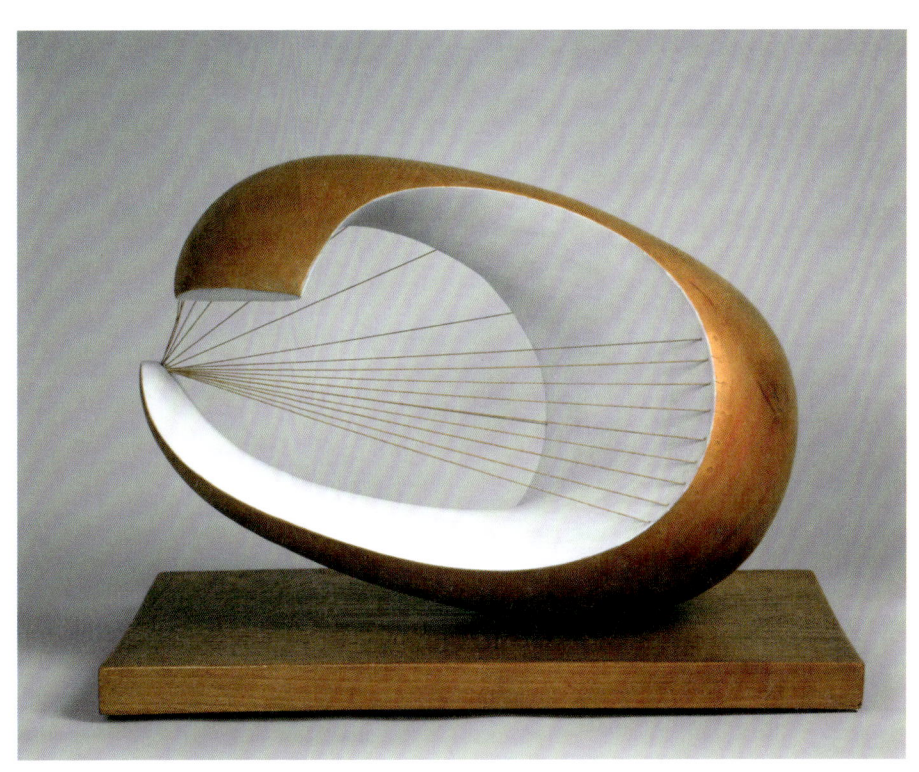

Wave 1943–4
Plane wood, paint and strings
30.5 × 44.5 × 21

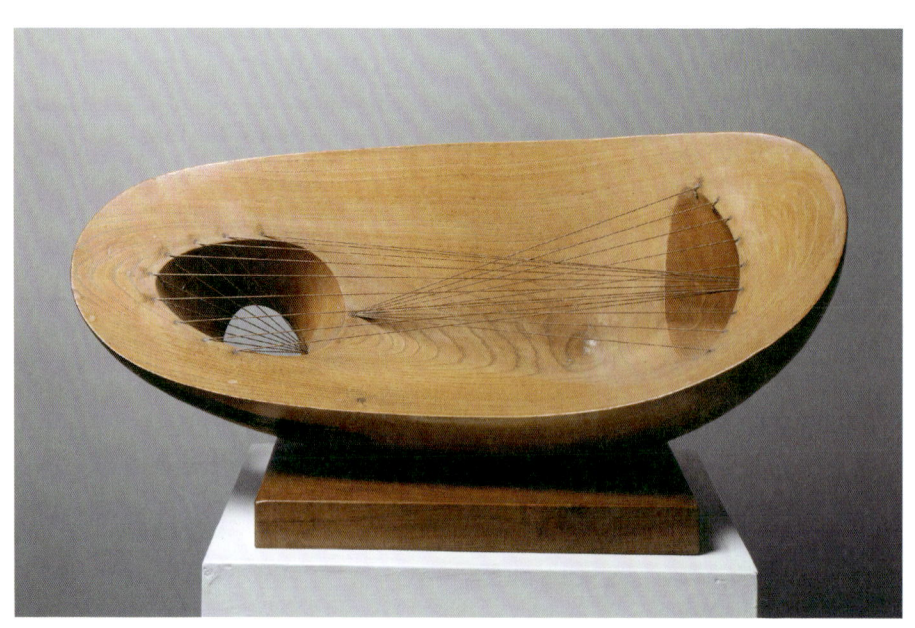

Landscape Sculpture 1944
Elm wood and strings
32 × 68 × 29

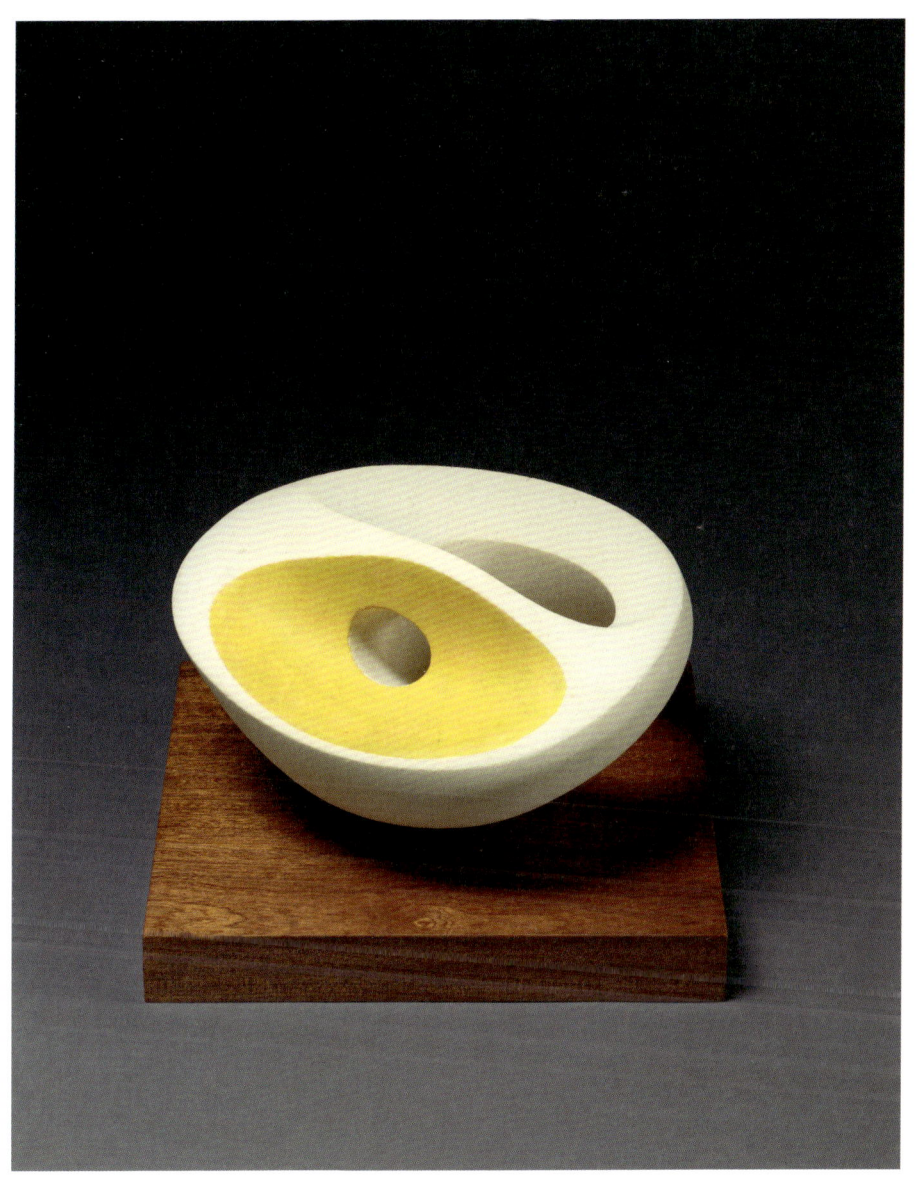

Curved Stone with Yellow 1946
Stone and paint
18 × 27 × 26

Project for Waterloo Bridge:
The Sea 1947
Oil paint, watercolour,
crayon and graphite
on paper
46.4 × 59

Model for Project for
Waterloo Bridge: The River
1947
Portland stone
10 × 20.8 × 6.6

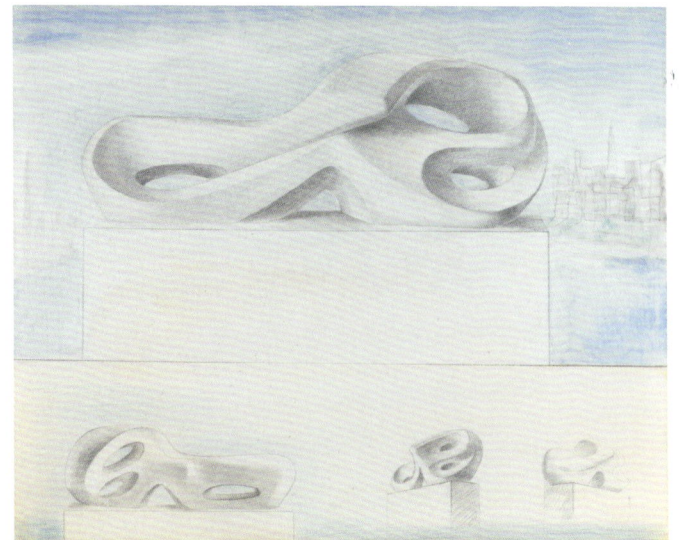

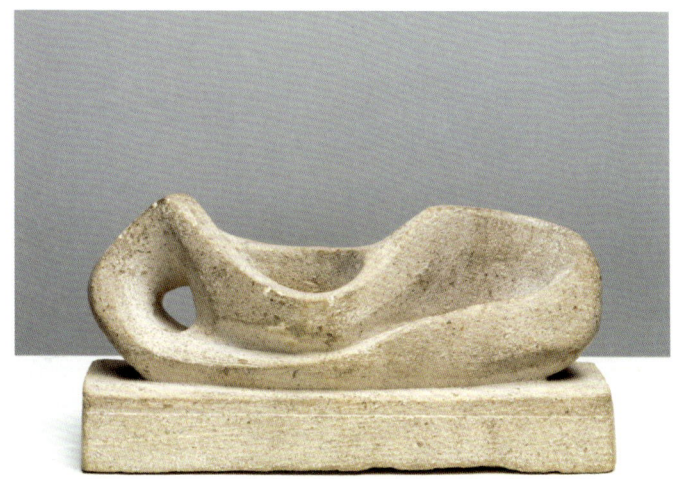

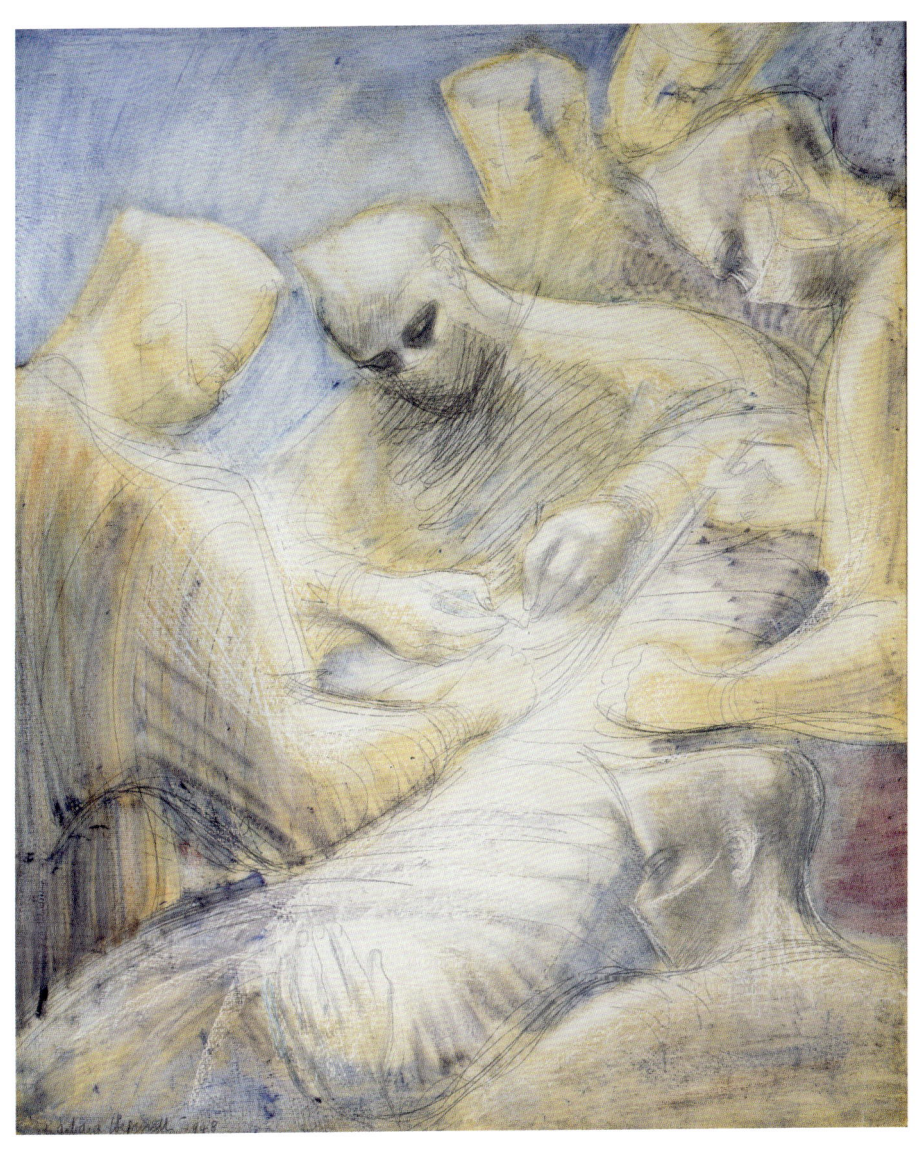

Quartet 'Arthroplasty' 1948
Oil paint and graphite
on board
59.6 × 50

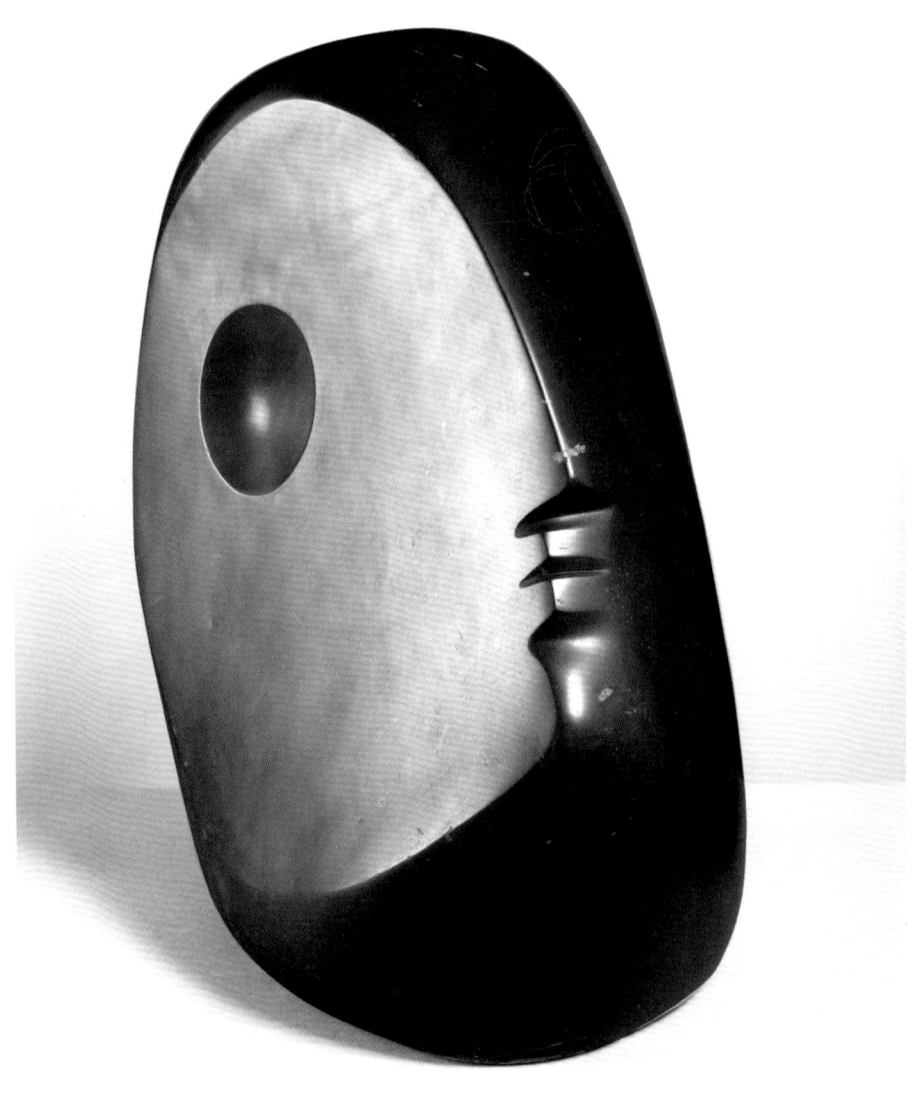

The Cosdon Head 1949
Blue marble
63.5 × 36.5 × 54

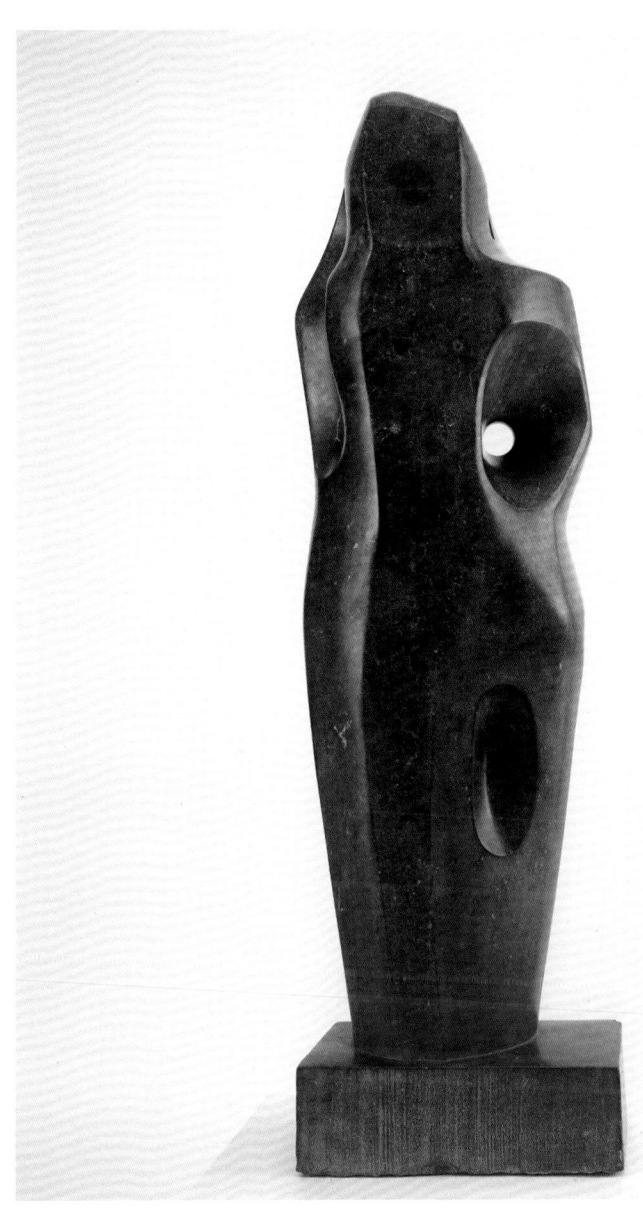

Bicentric Form 1949
Limestone
159 × 52.2 × 33

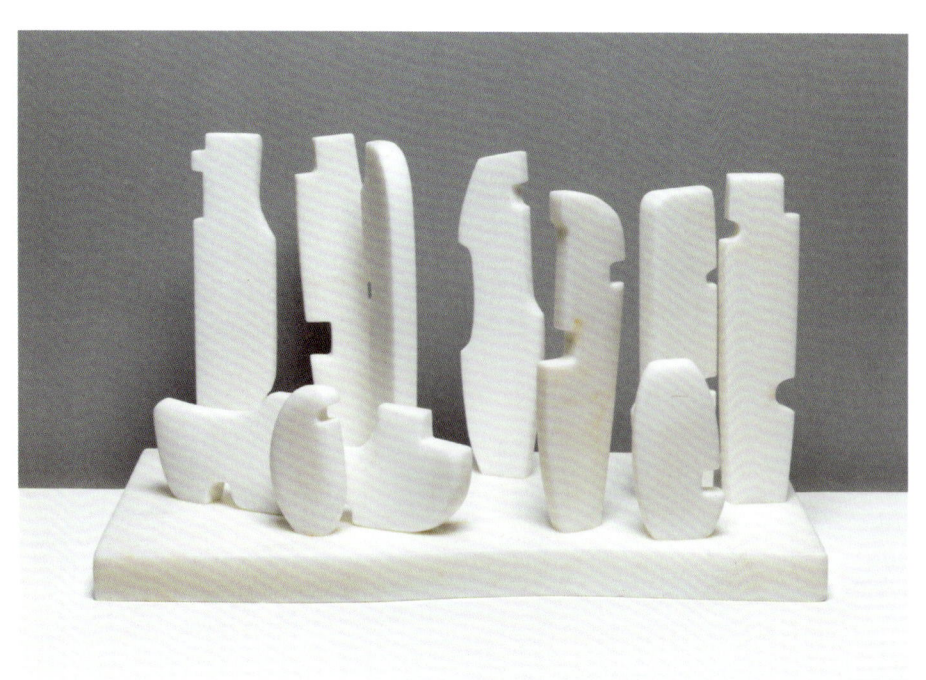

Group II (People Waiting) 1952
Seravezza marble
25.5 × 50.7 × 29

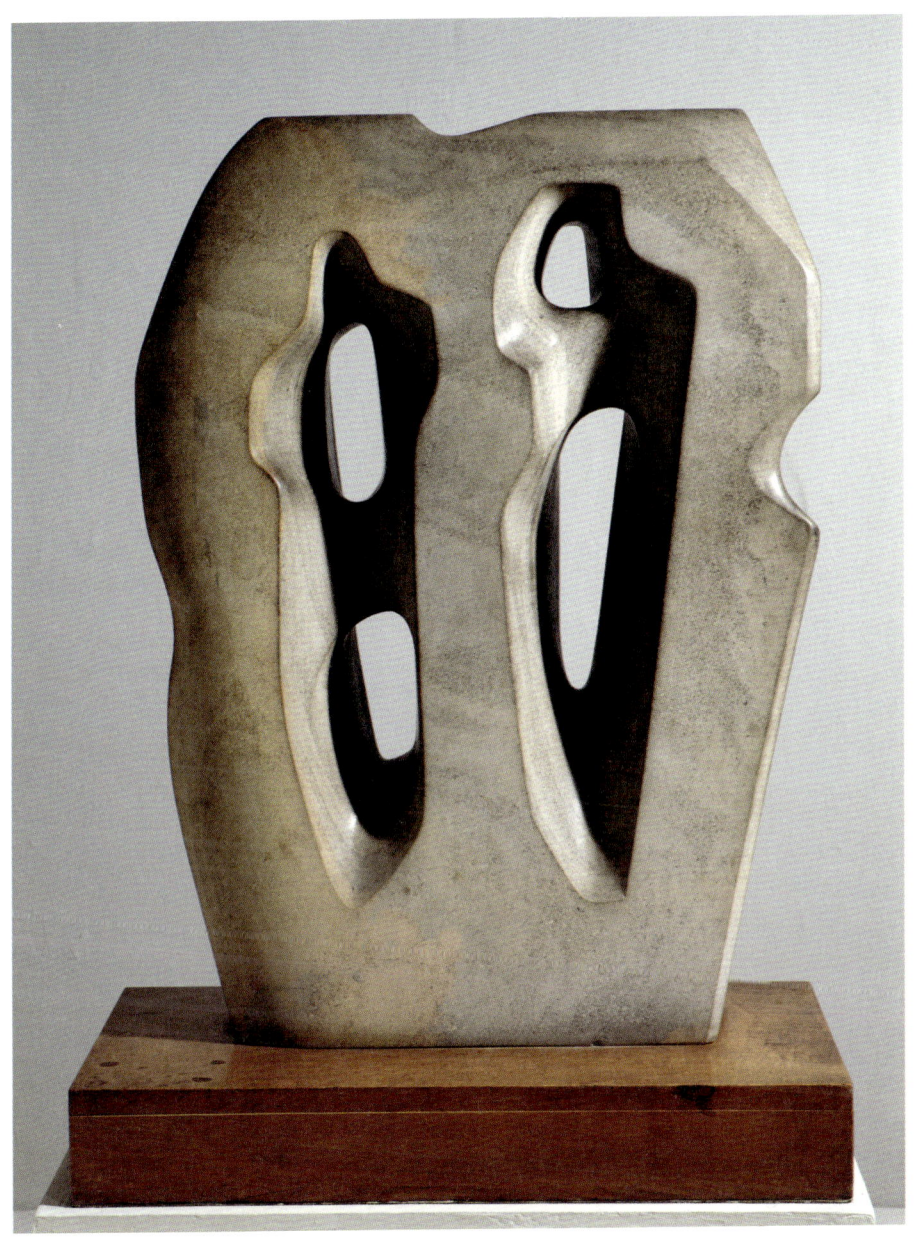

Hieroglyph 1953
Ancaster stone
101.8 × 86 × 45 (excl. base)

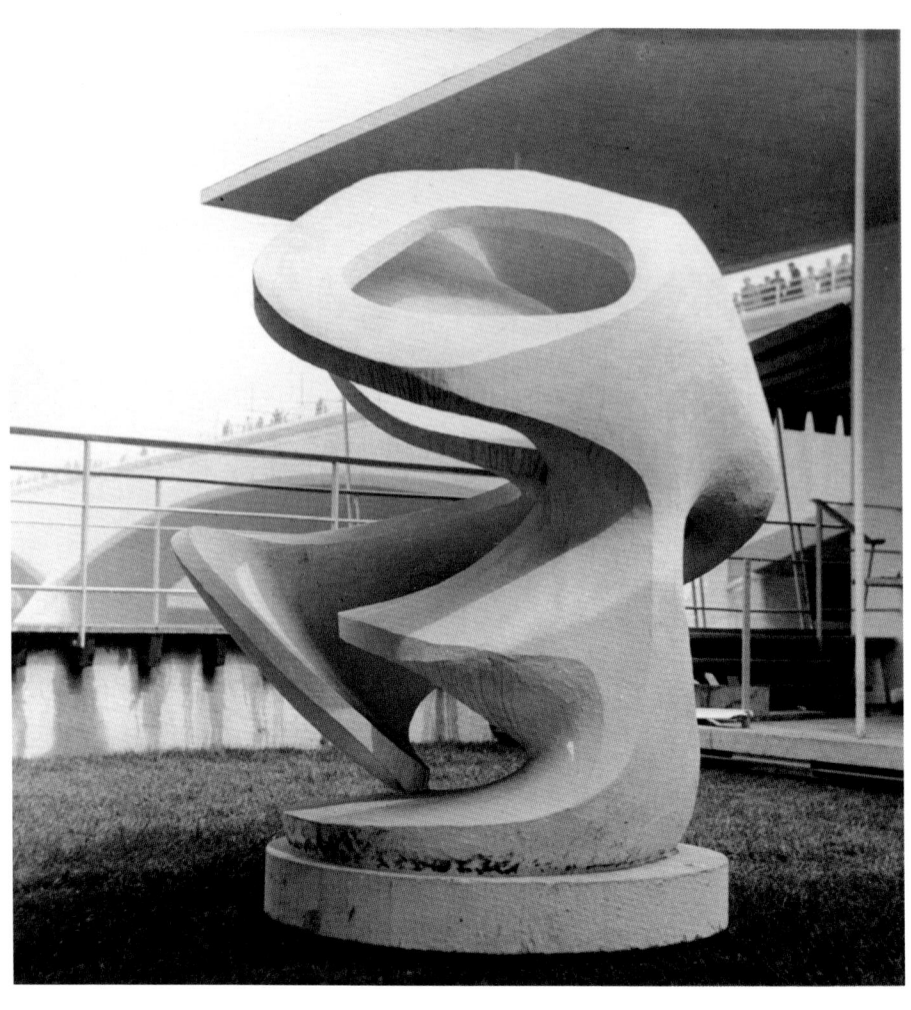

Turning Forms 1950–1
Reinforced concrete with Snowcrete and
Snowcem
213 high
In situ at the Festival Britain, South Bank
site, Lambeth, London, photograph 1951

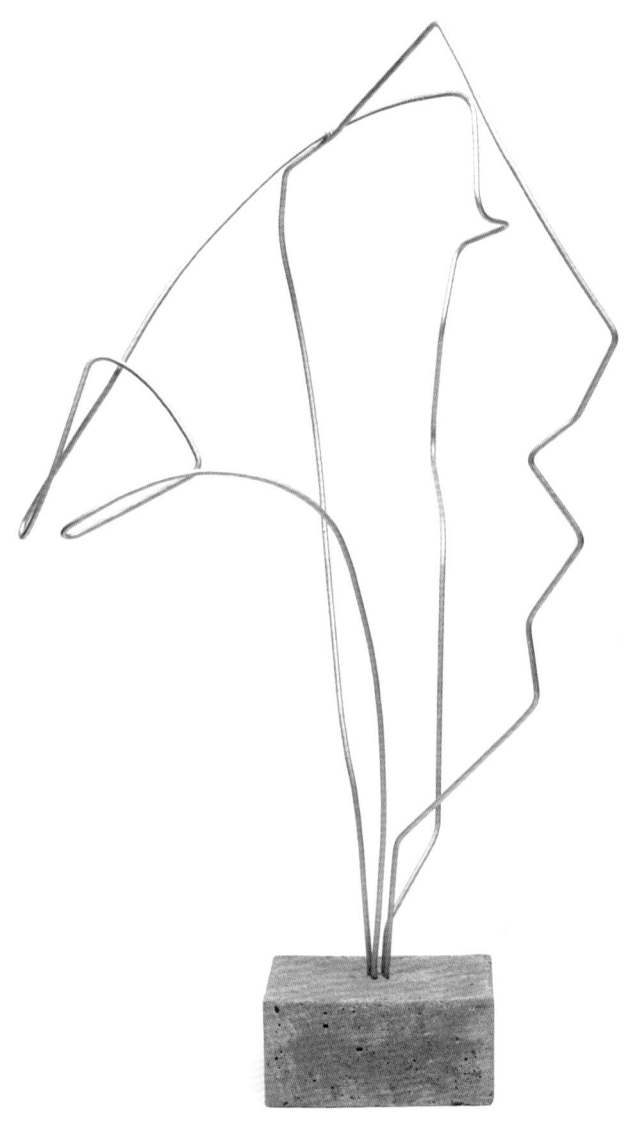

Apollo 1951
Painted steel rod
173.5 × 102 × 84

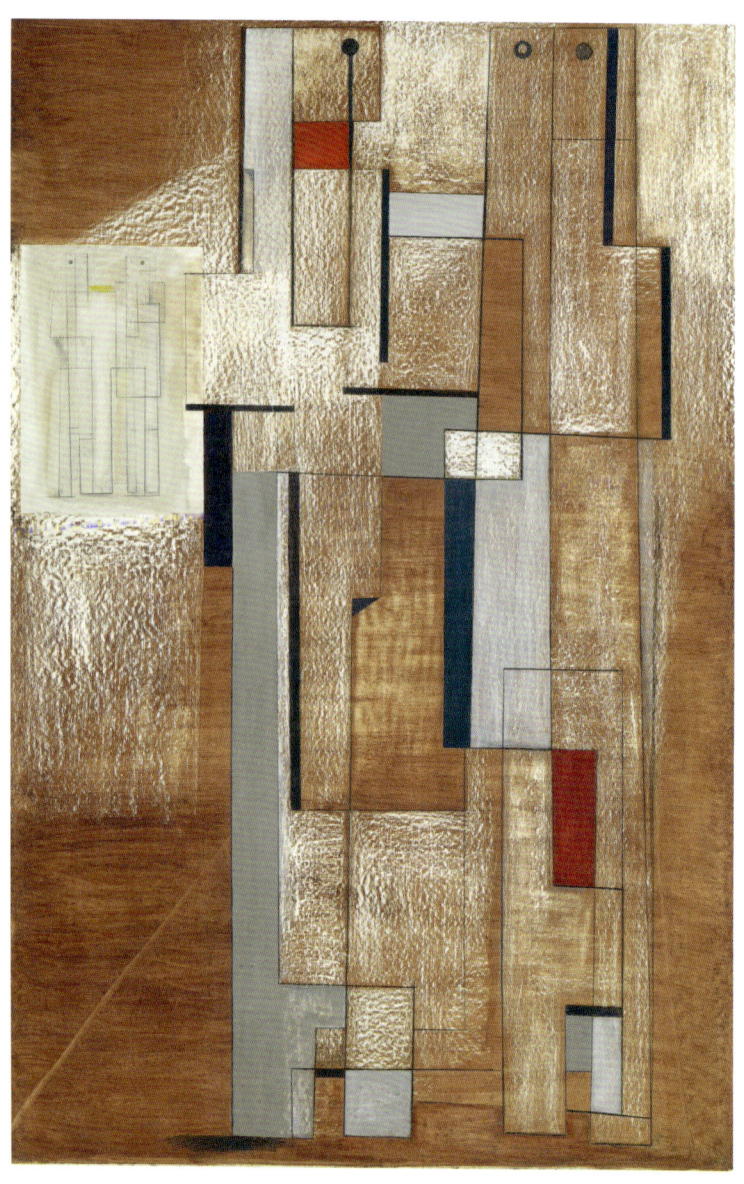

Two Figures (Heroes) 1954
Oil paint and graphite on
board
185 × 122

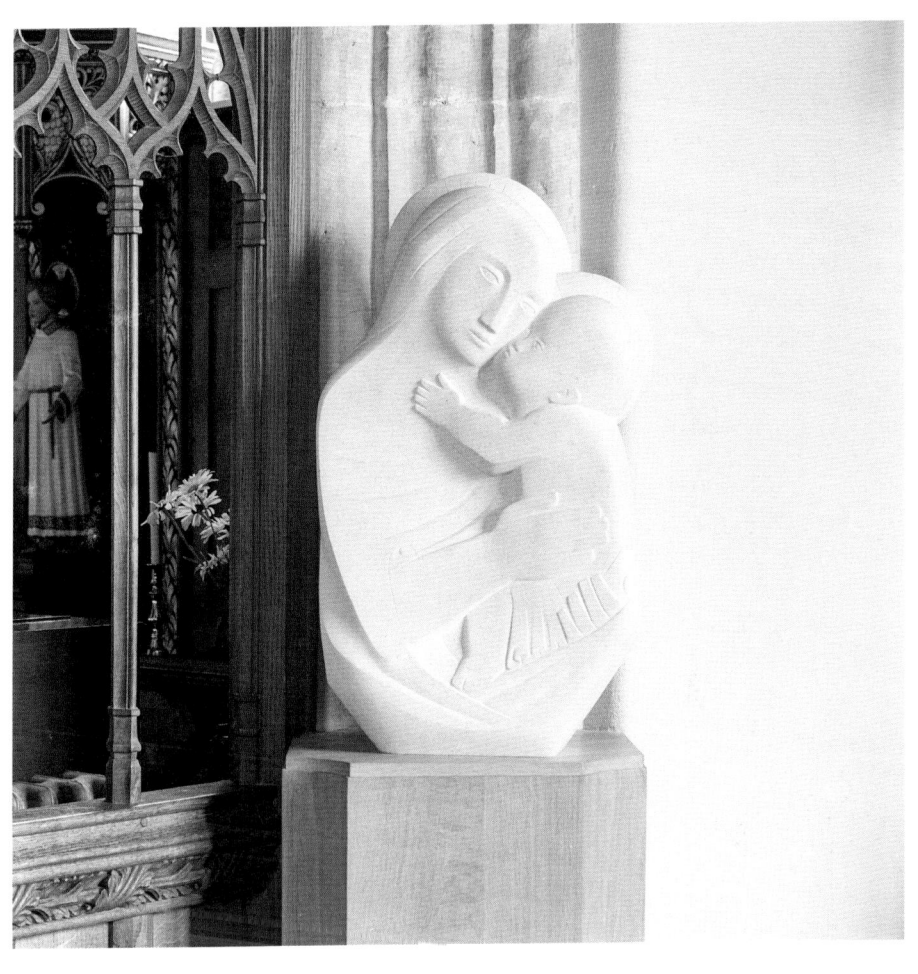

Madonna and Child 1954
Bianco del mare
79 x 44.5 x 26.7
In situ in the Lady Chapel at the Church of St Ia,
St Ives, photograph 1956

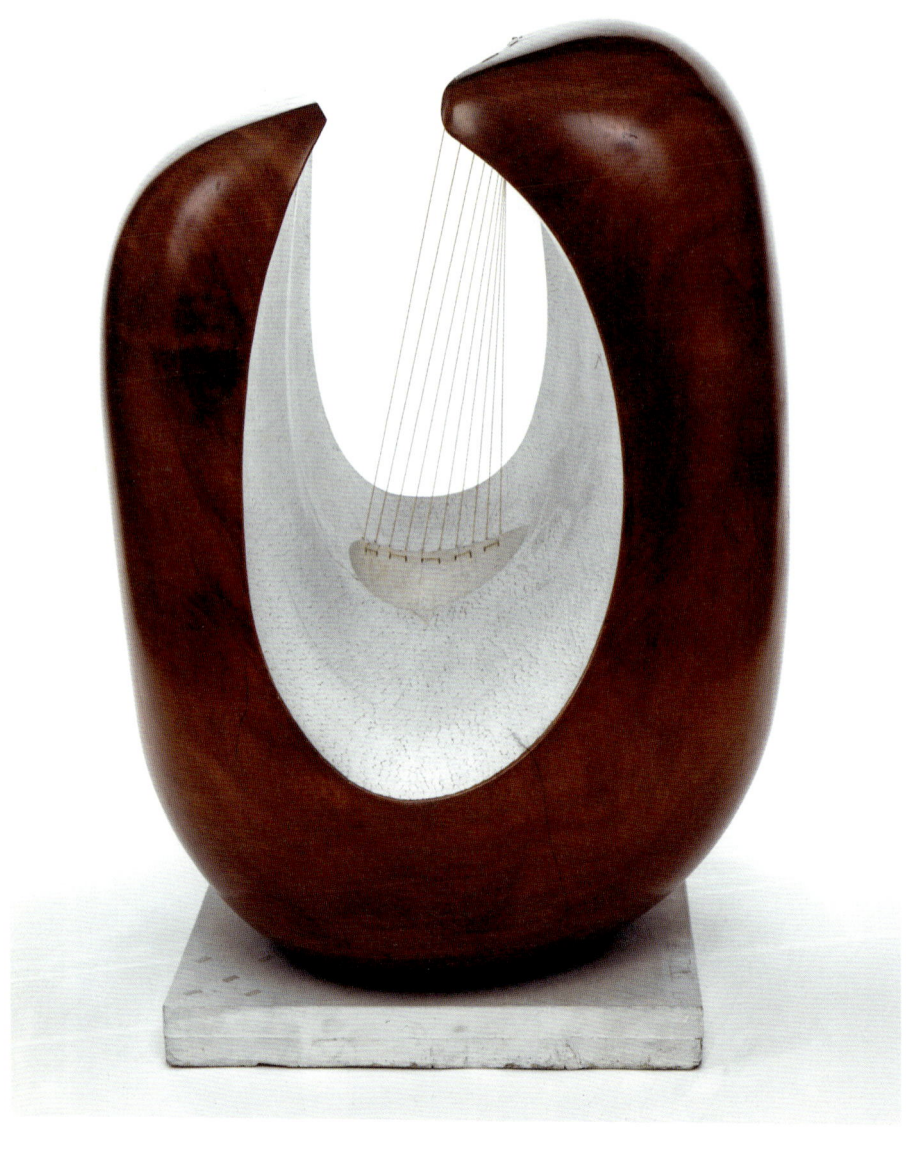

Curved Form (Delphi) 1955
Guarea wood, string and
paint on wooden base
102 × 74 × 77

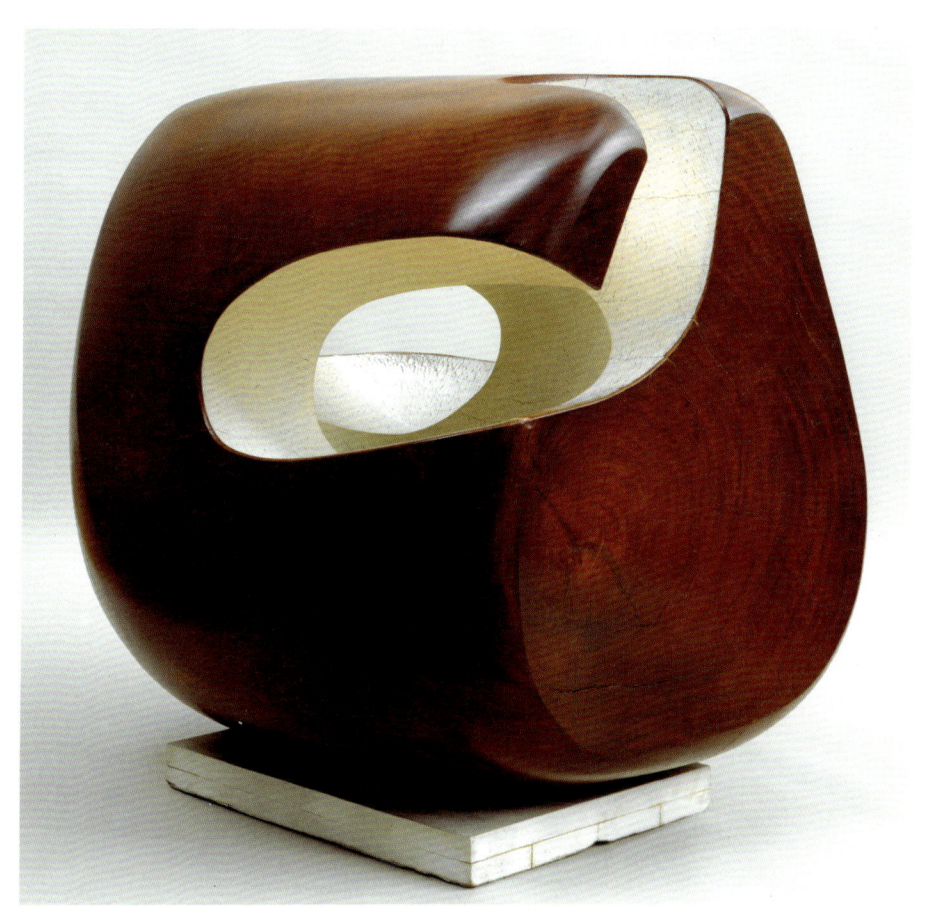

Corinthos 1954–5
Guarea wood and paint on
wooden base
104.1 × 10.67 × 101.6

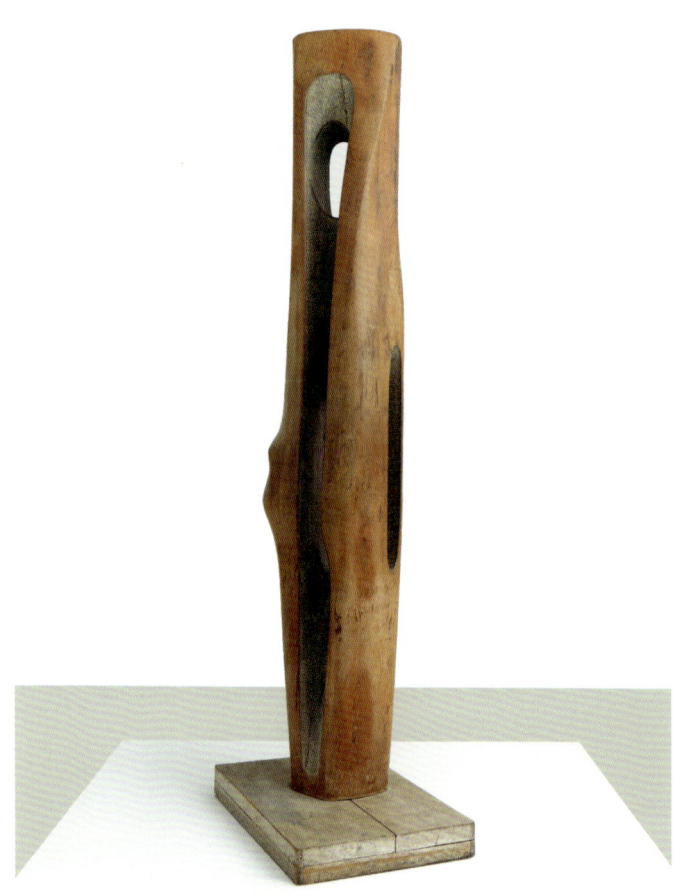

Figure (Nanjizal) 1958
Yew on oakwood base
246.9 × 45.7 × 33 (excl. base)

Pierced Form (Epidauros) 1960
Guarea wood and paint
74 × 67.6 × 36

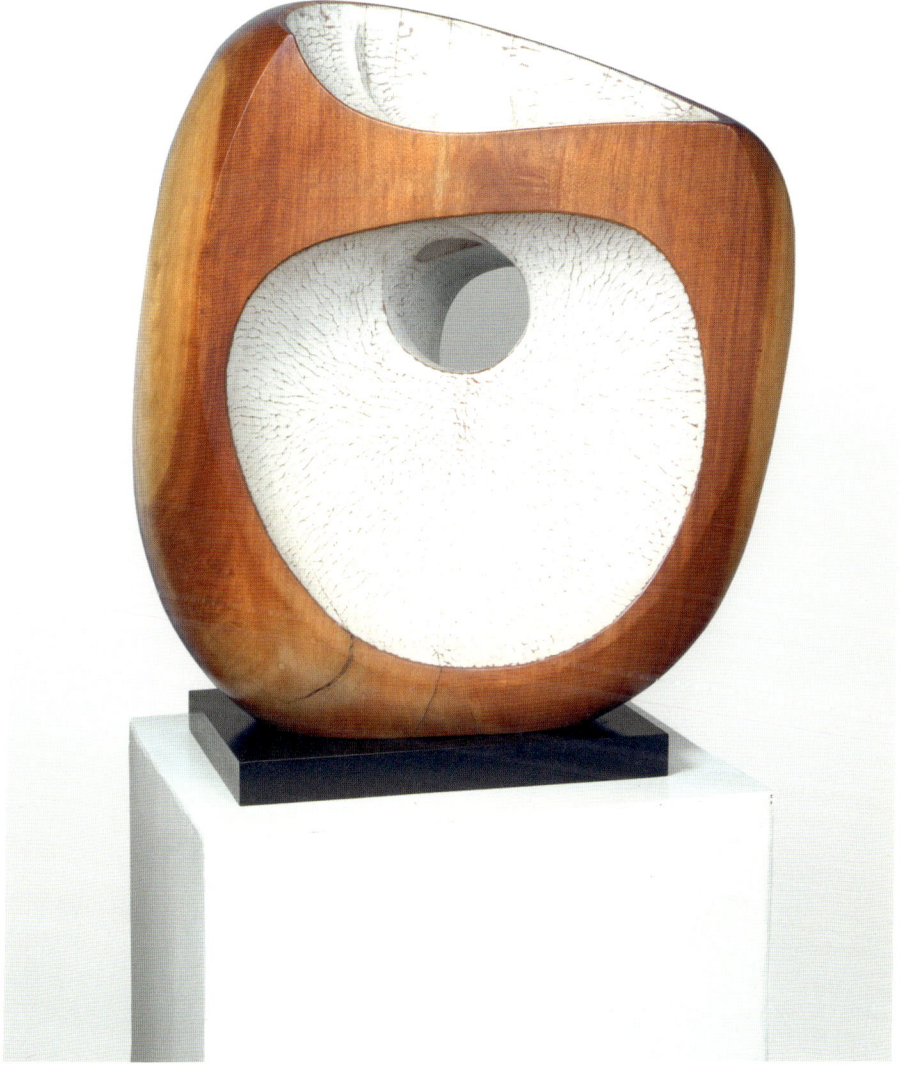

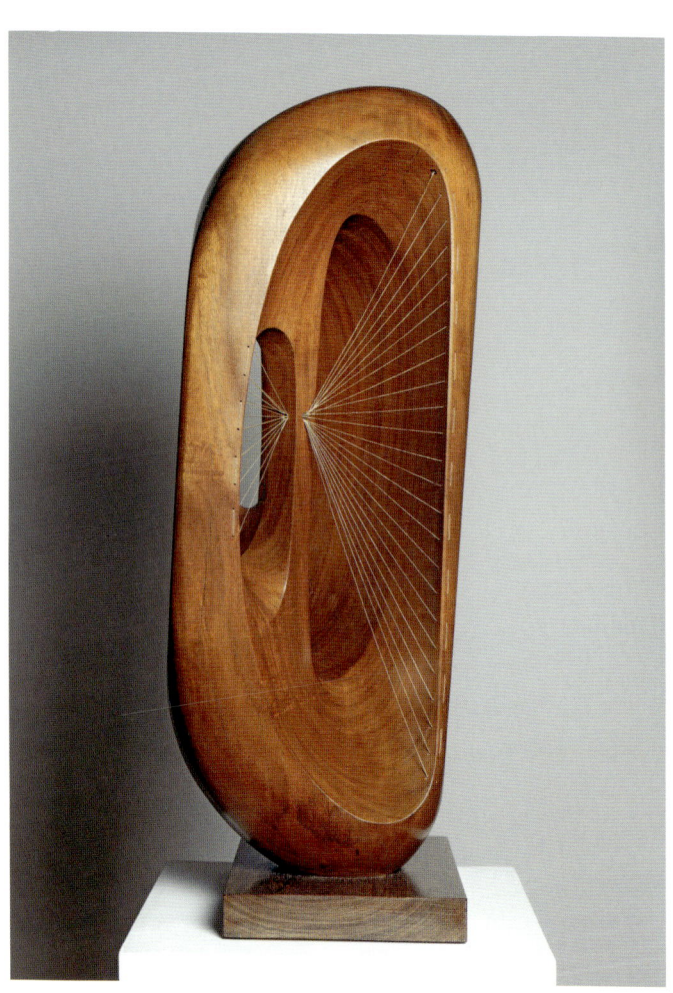

Fugue 1956
Mahogany and strings
78 high

Orpheus (Maquette 1) 1956
Brass and string
42.4 x 15 x 26 (excl. base)

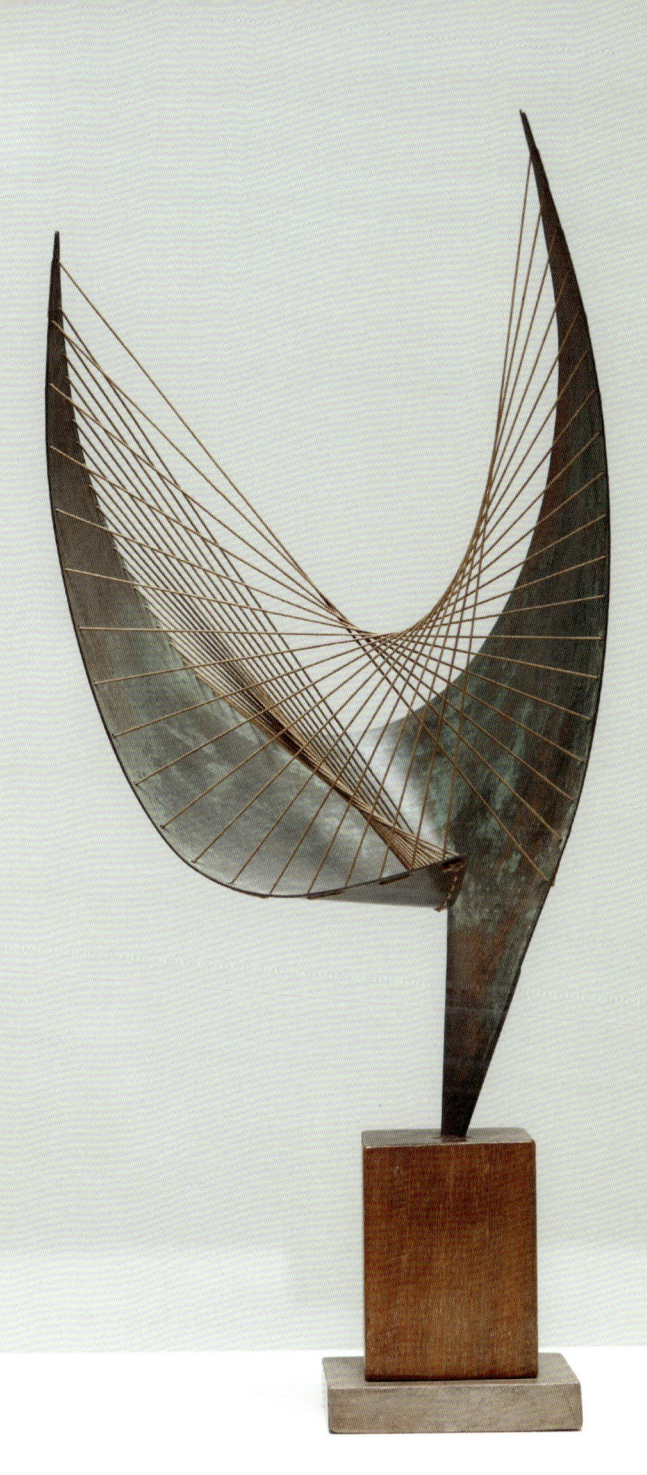

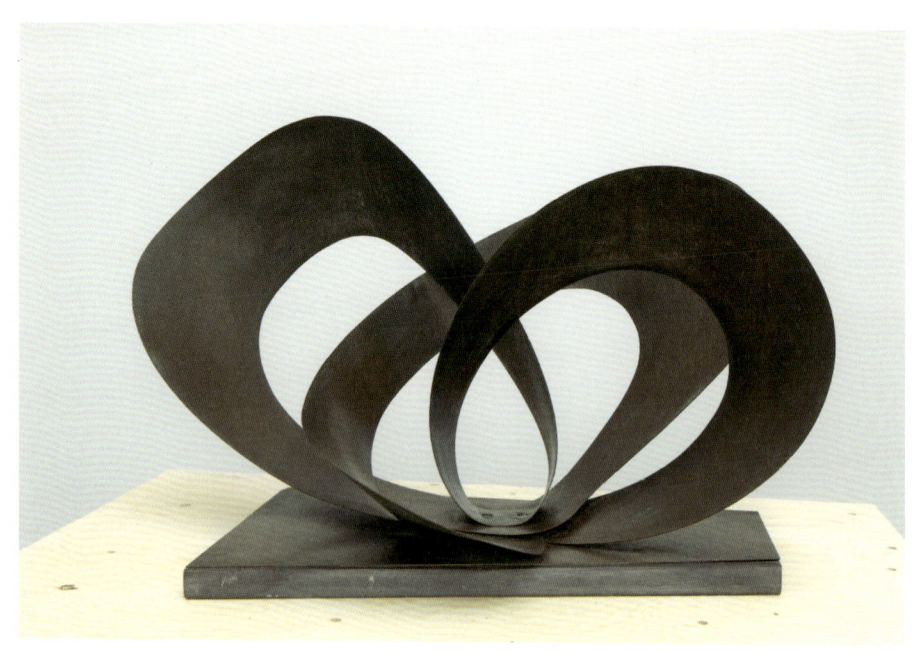

Forms in Movement
(Galliard) 1956
Copper
50 × 85 × 52

Spring (Project for Sculpture)
1957
Oil paint and ink on board
61 × 45.6

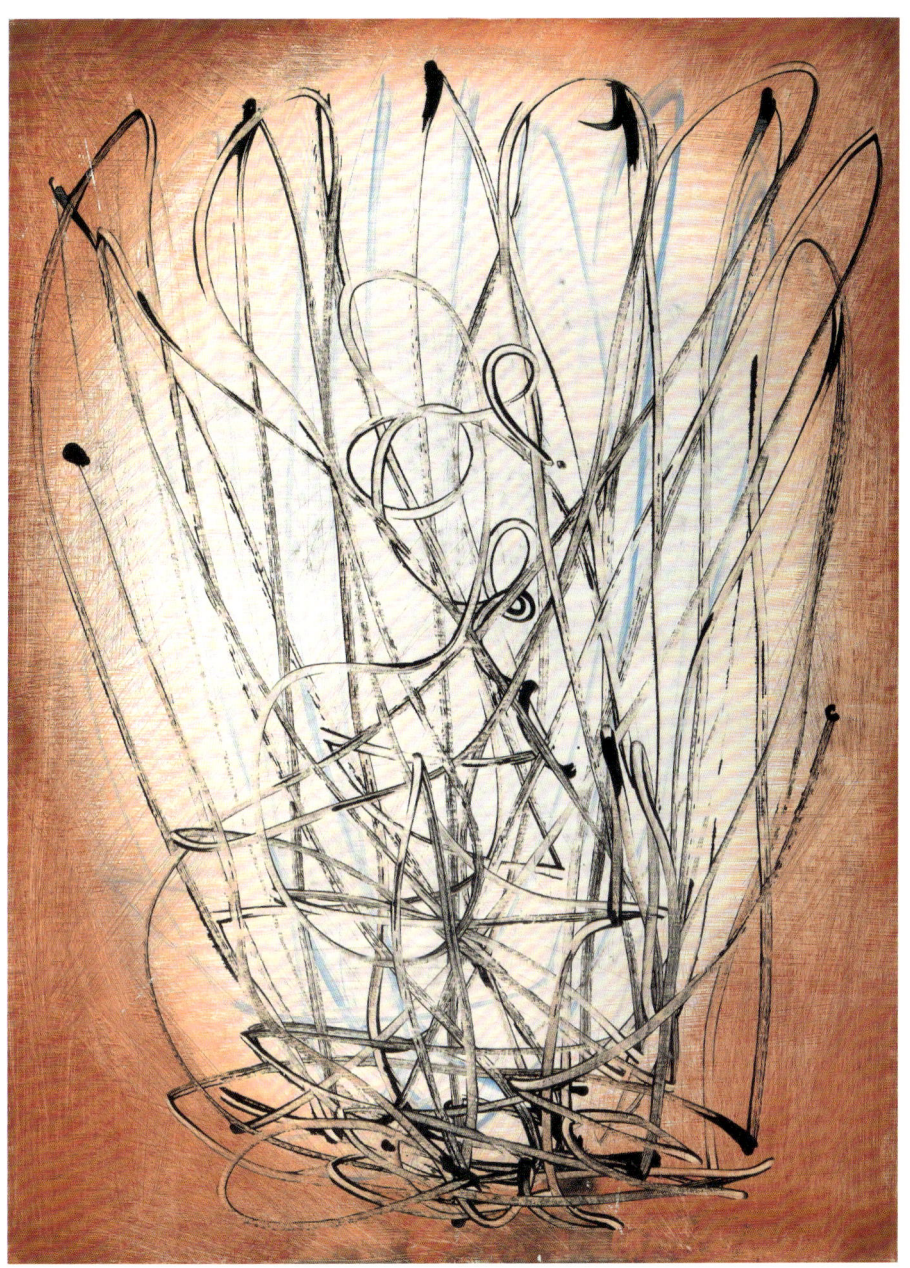

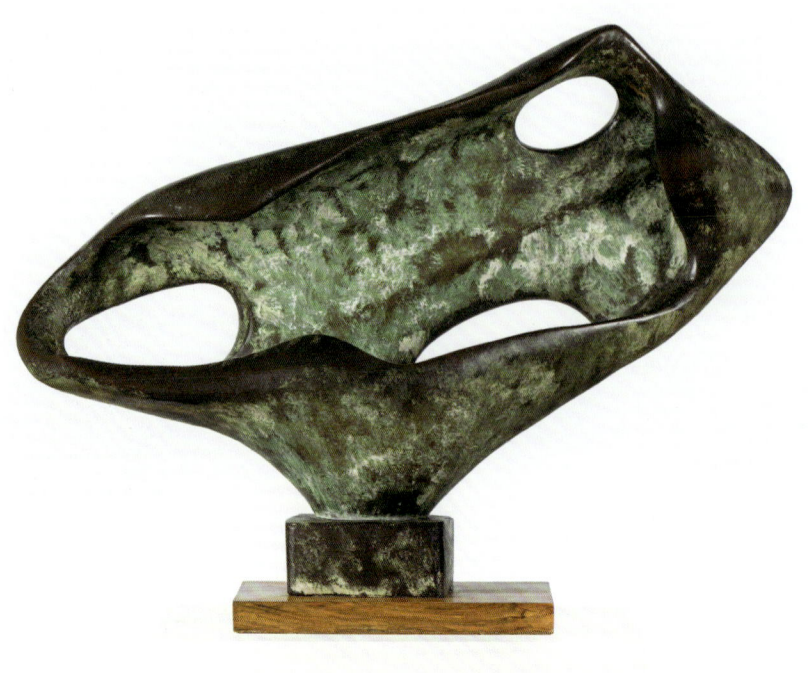

Sea Form (Porthmeor) 1958
Bronze
83 x 113.5 x 35.5

Curved Form (Trevalgan) 1956
Bronze
90.2 x 59.7 x 67.3

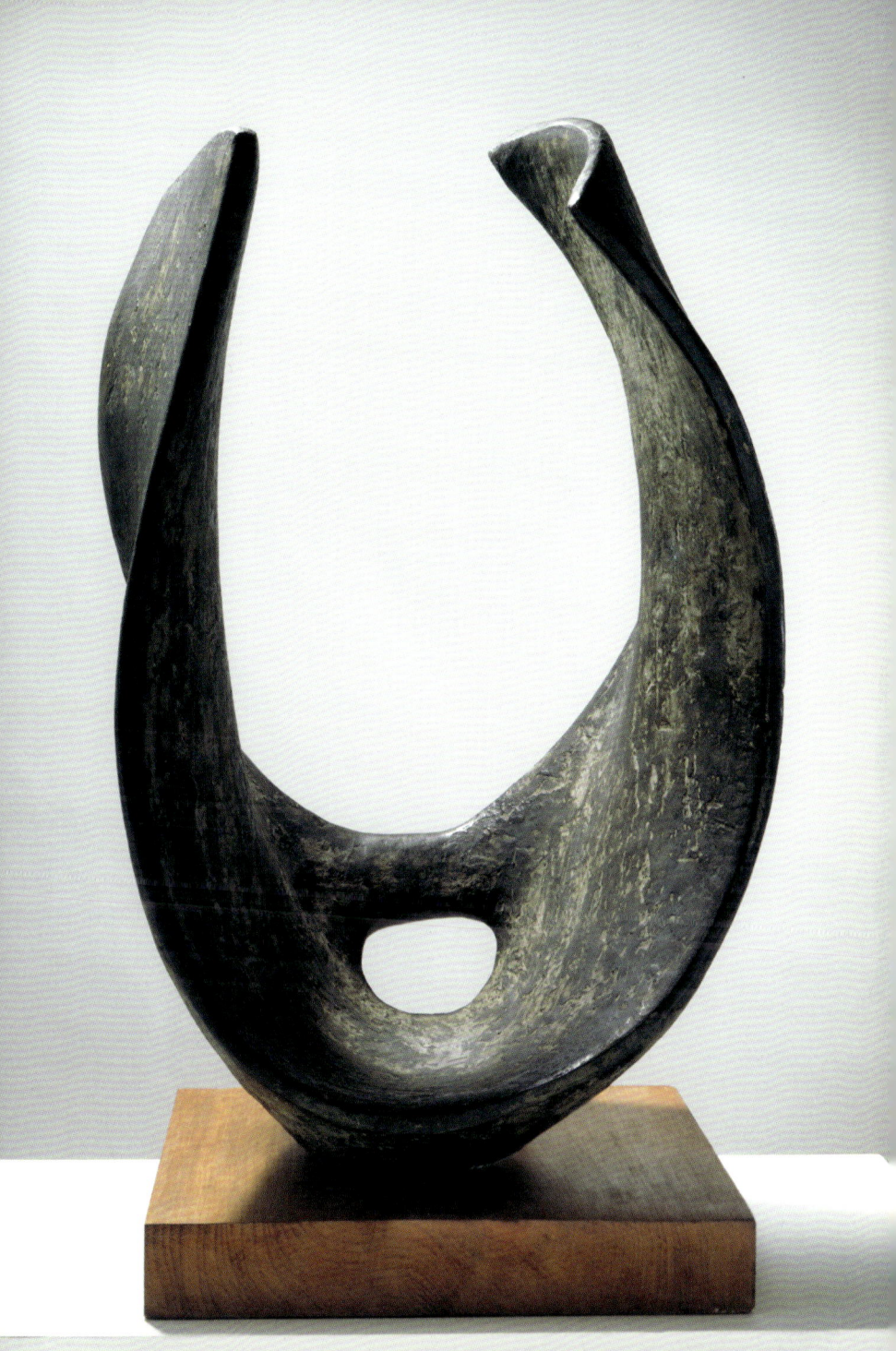

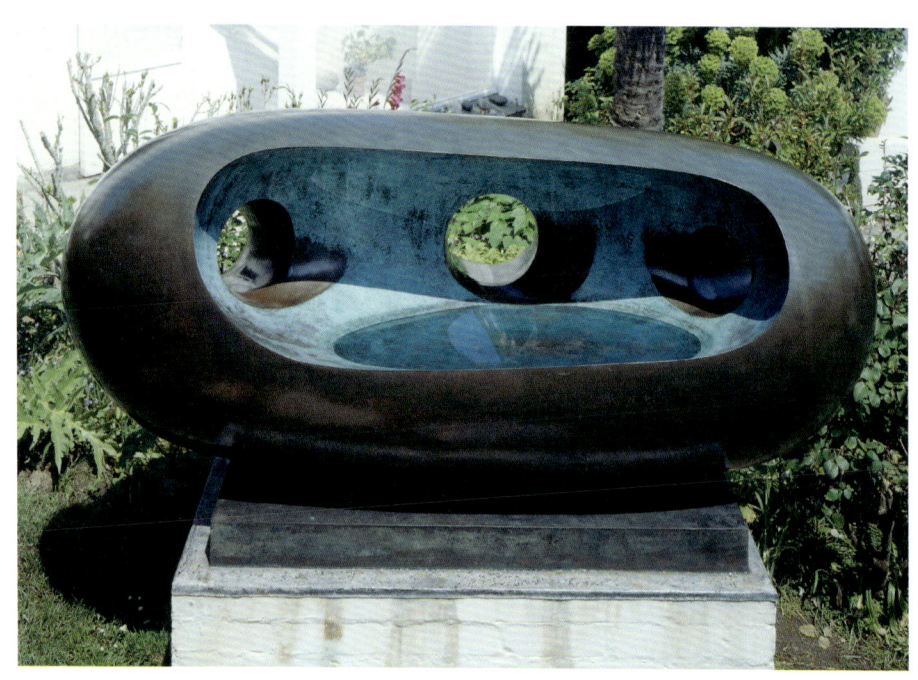

River Form 1965
Bronze
87 × 190 × 85
Installation view in the Barbara Hepworth
Museum and Garden, St Ives

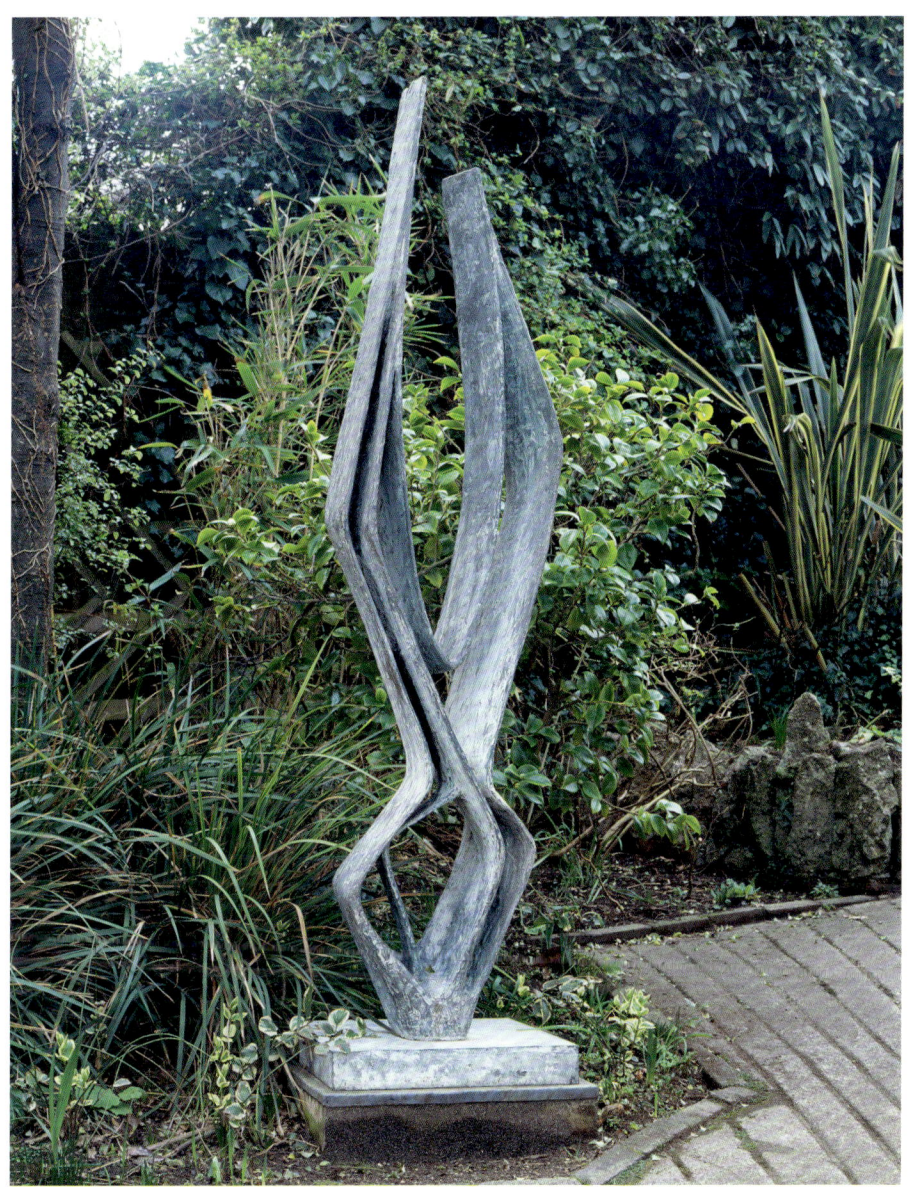

Cantate Domino 1958
Bronze
209.5 x 53 x 50.5
Installation view in the Barbara Hepworth
Museum and Garden, St Ives

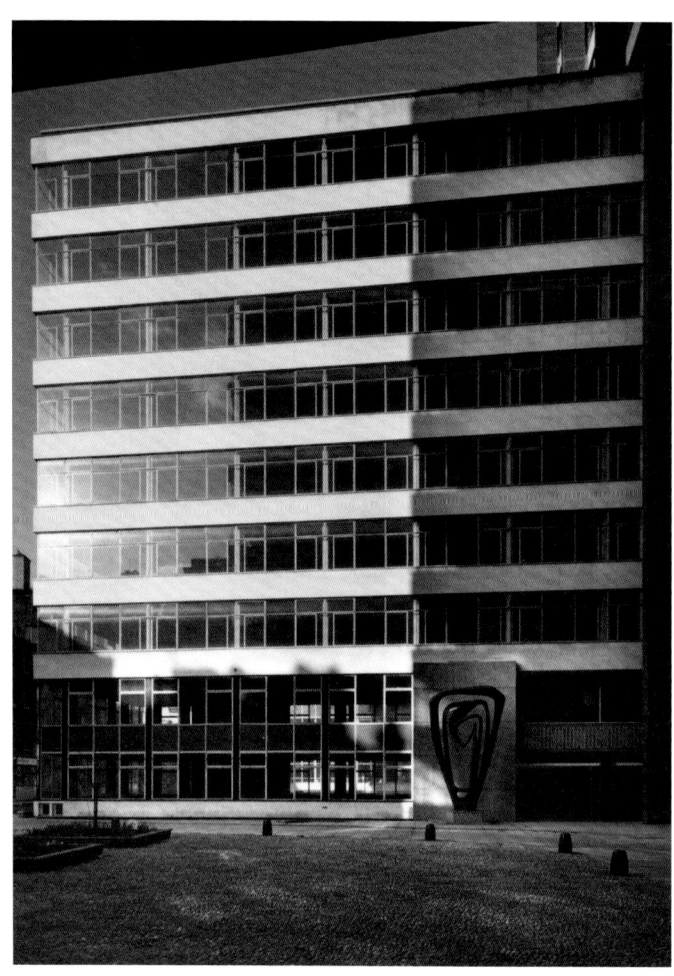

Meridian, Sculpture for State
House 1958–60
Bronze
460 high
In situ at State House,
High Holborn, London,
photograph 1961

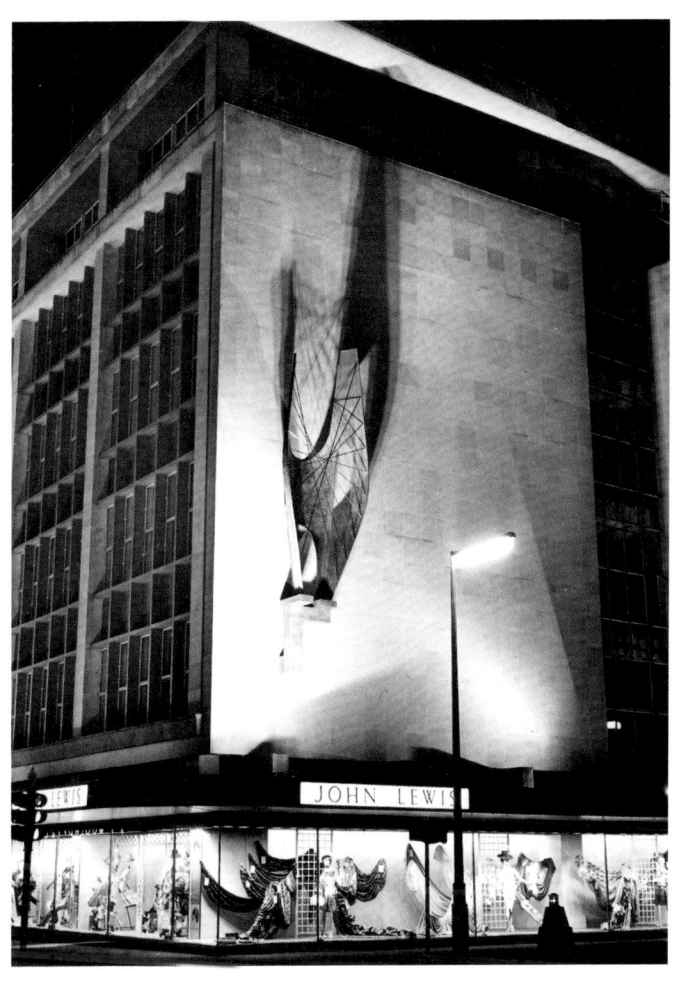

Winged Figure 1961–3
Aluminium and steel rods
586.5 x 254 x 159.5 (excl. base)
In situ upon the facade of John
Lewis, Oxford Street, London,
photograph 1963

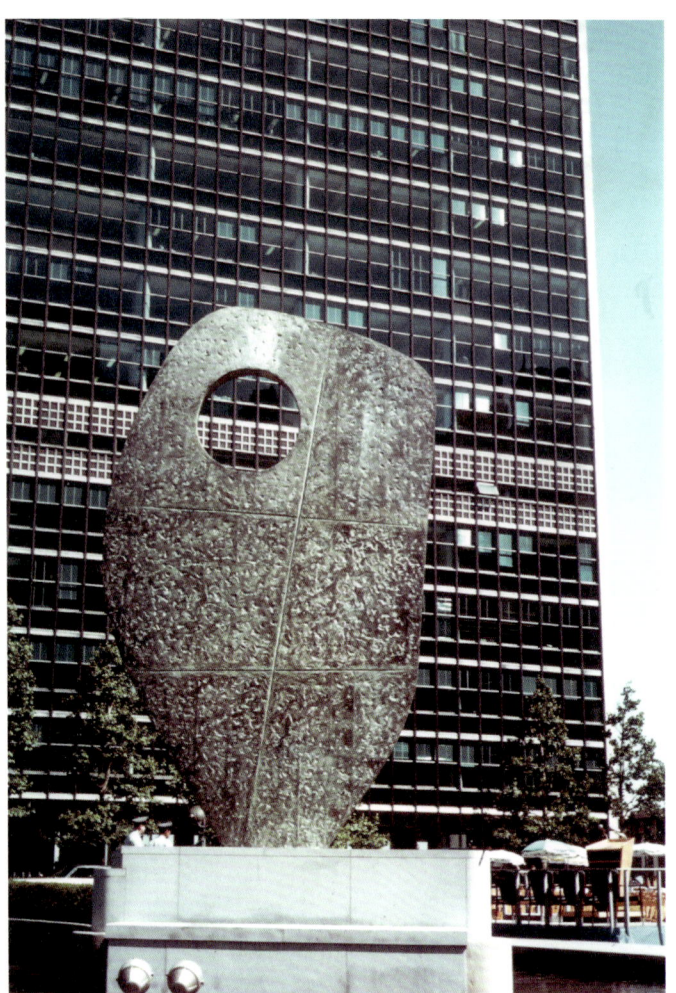

Single Form 1961–4
Bronze
640 high
In situ at the United Nations,
New York, photograph 1964

Single Form (September) 1961
Walnut
82.5 × 50.8 × 5.7

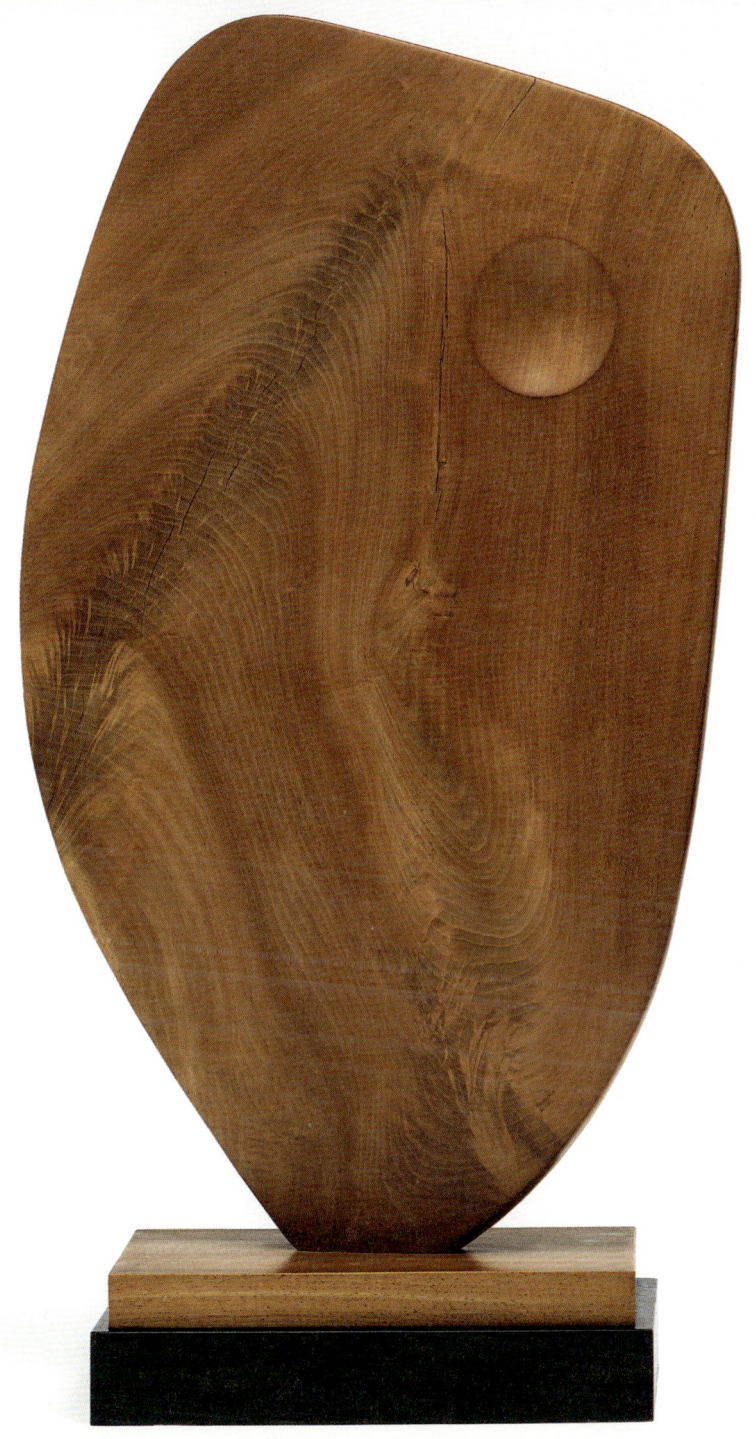

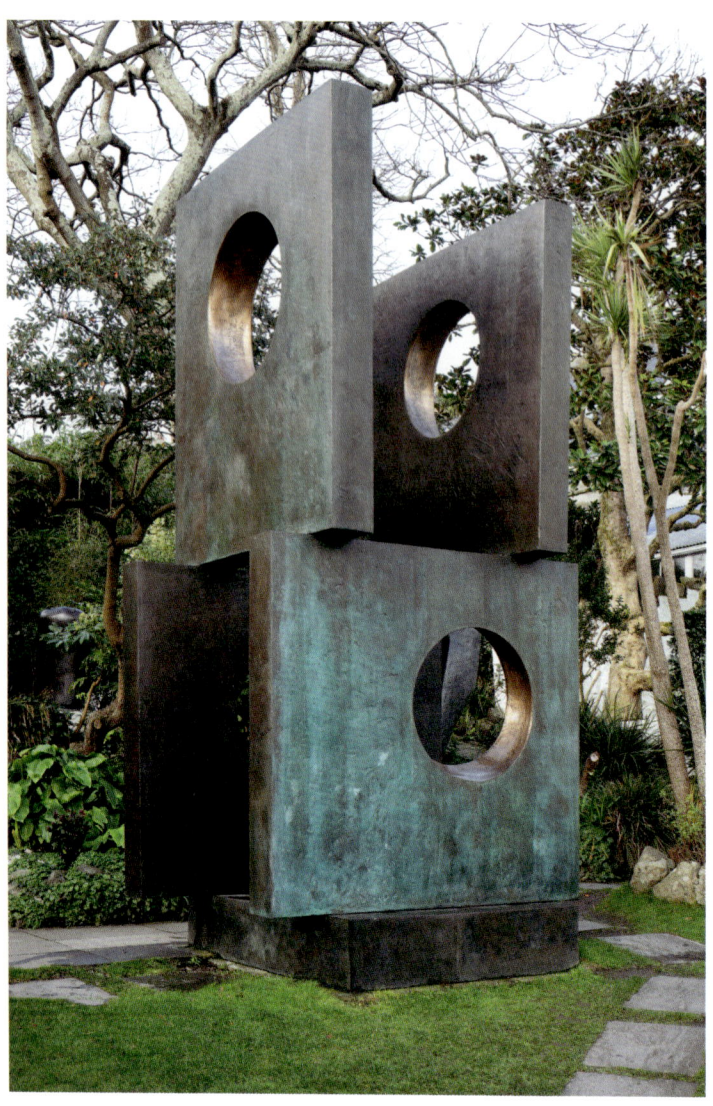

Four-Square (Walk Through) 1966
Bronze
425 × 197 × 229
Installation view in the Barbara Hepworth
Museum and Garden, St Ives

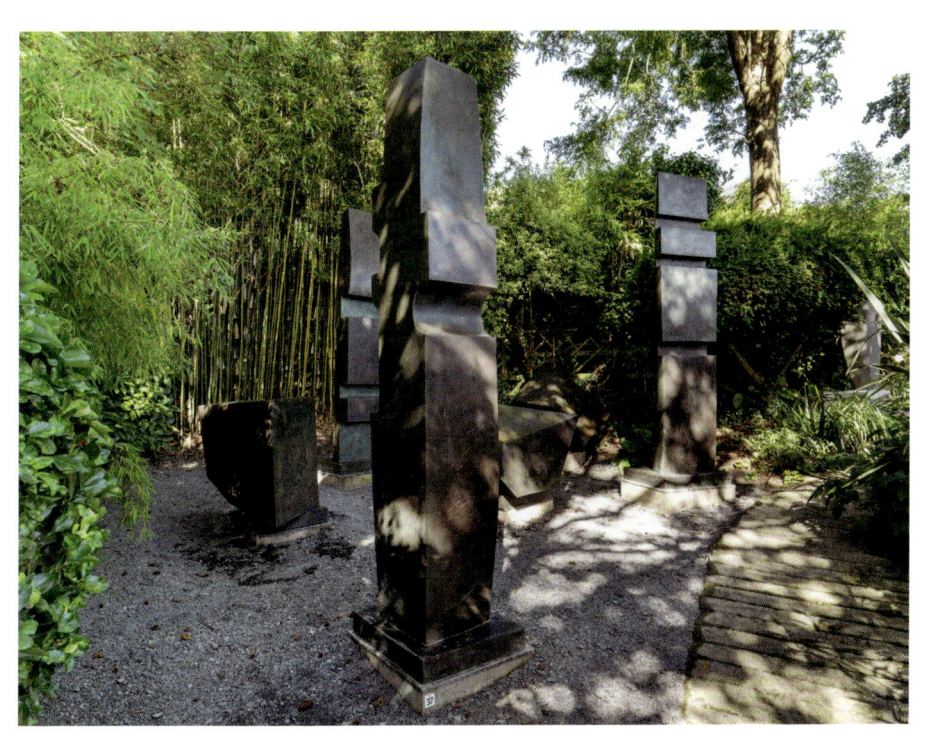

Conversation with Magic Stones 1973
Bronze, six parts
269.2 × 63.5 × 45.7; 274.3 × 58.4 × 47; 282 ×
48.2 × 53.3; 80 × 130.8 × 91.4;
86.3 × 106.6 × 121.9; 92.7 × 121.9 × 60.9
Installation view in the Barbara Hepworth
Museum and Garden, St Ives

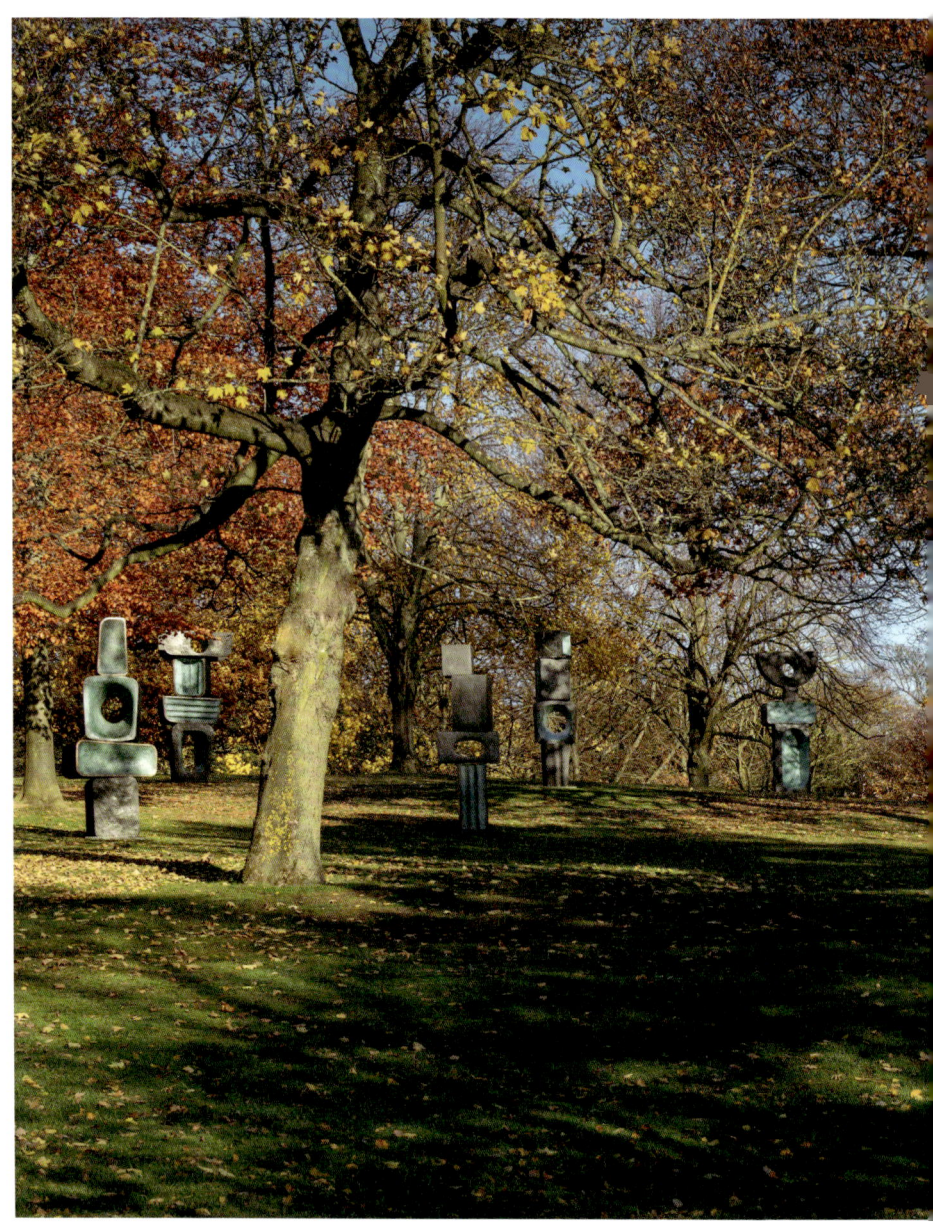

Family of Man 1970
Bronze, nine parts
300 high; 233 high; 268.8 high; 193 high; 276 high;
271.8 high; 240 high; 259 high; 171.5 high
Installation view in the Yorkshire Sculpture Park

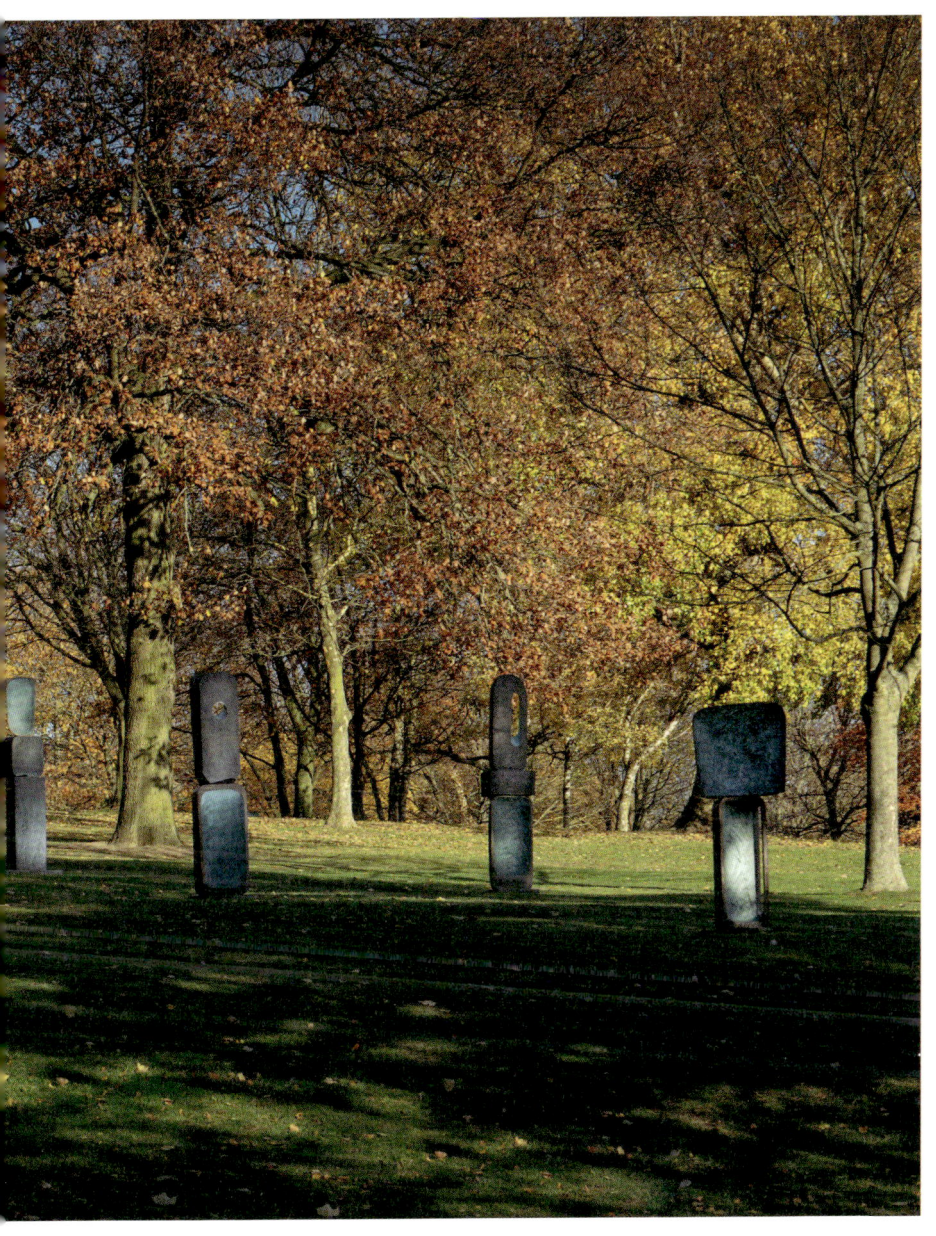

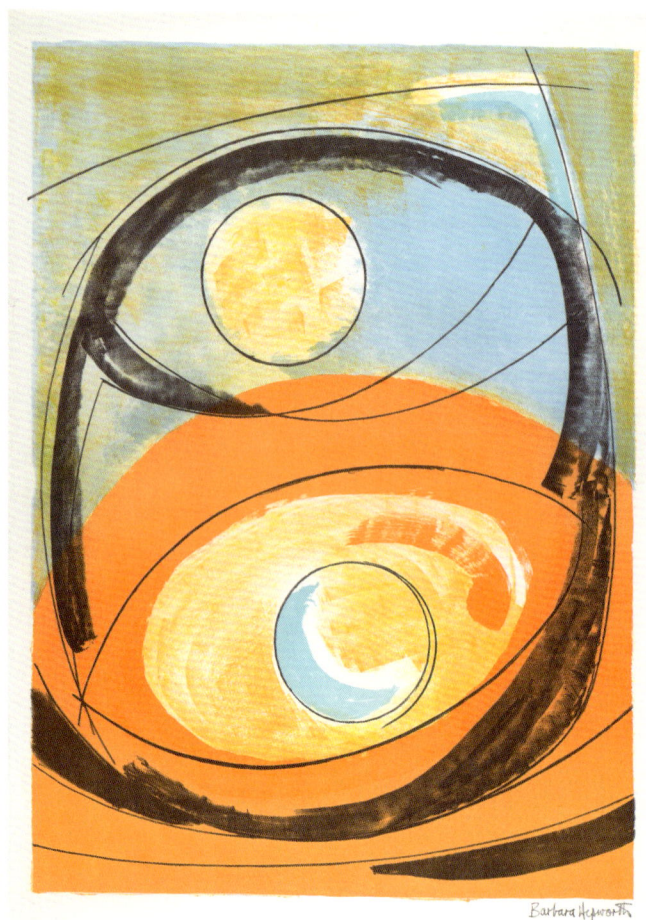

Barbara Hepworth

Genesis 1969
Lithograph on paper
72.4 × 53.7

Sun Setting (The Aegean
Suite) 1971
Lithograph on paper
75.6 × 54.5

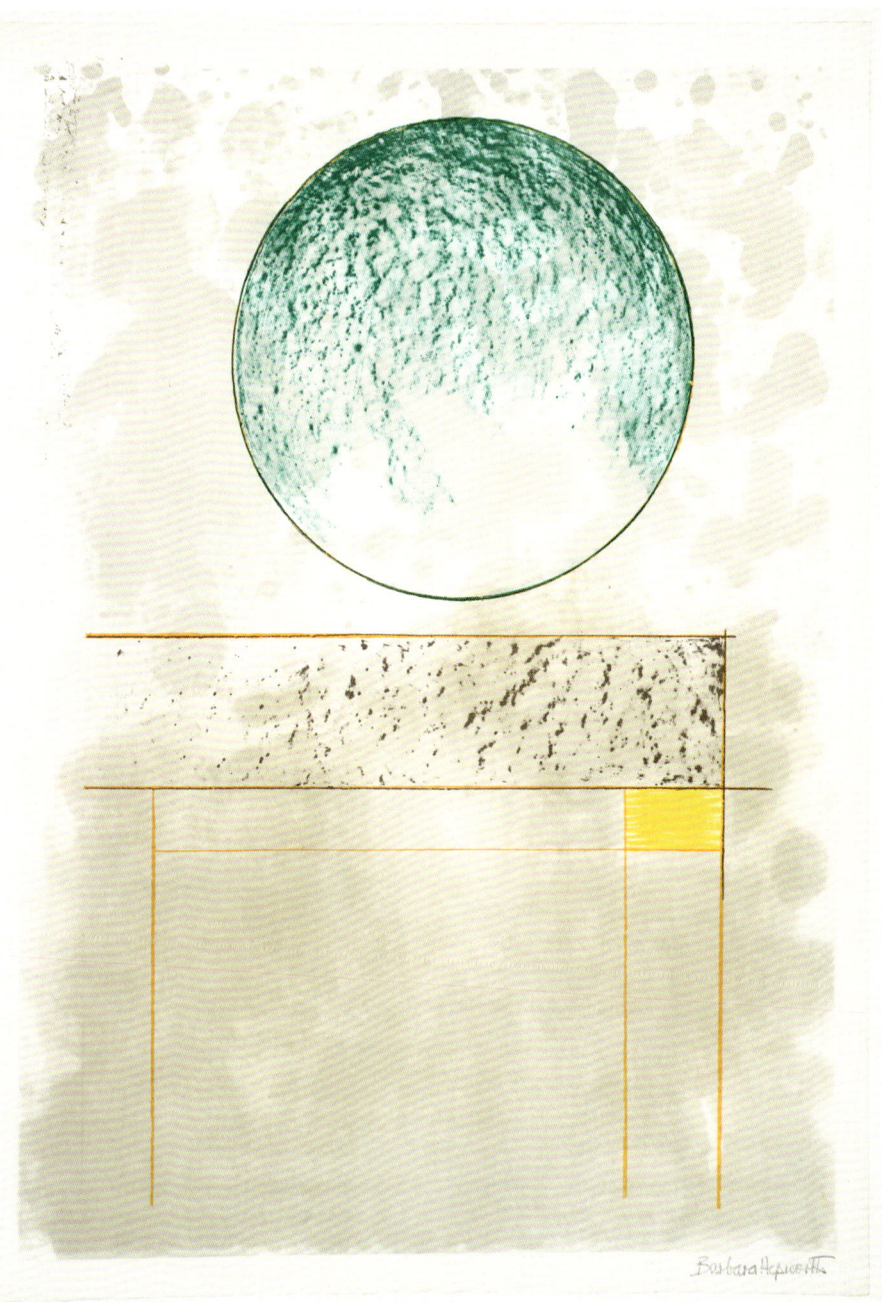

Barbara Hepworth

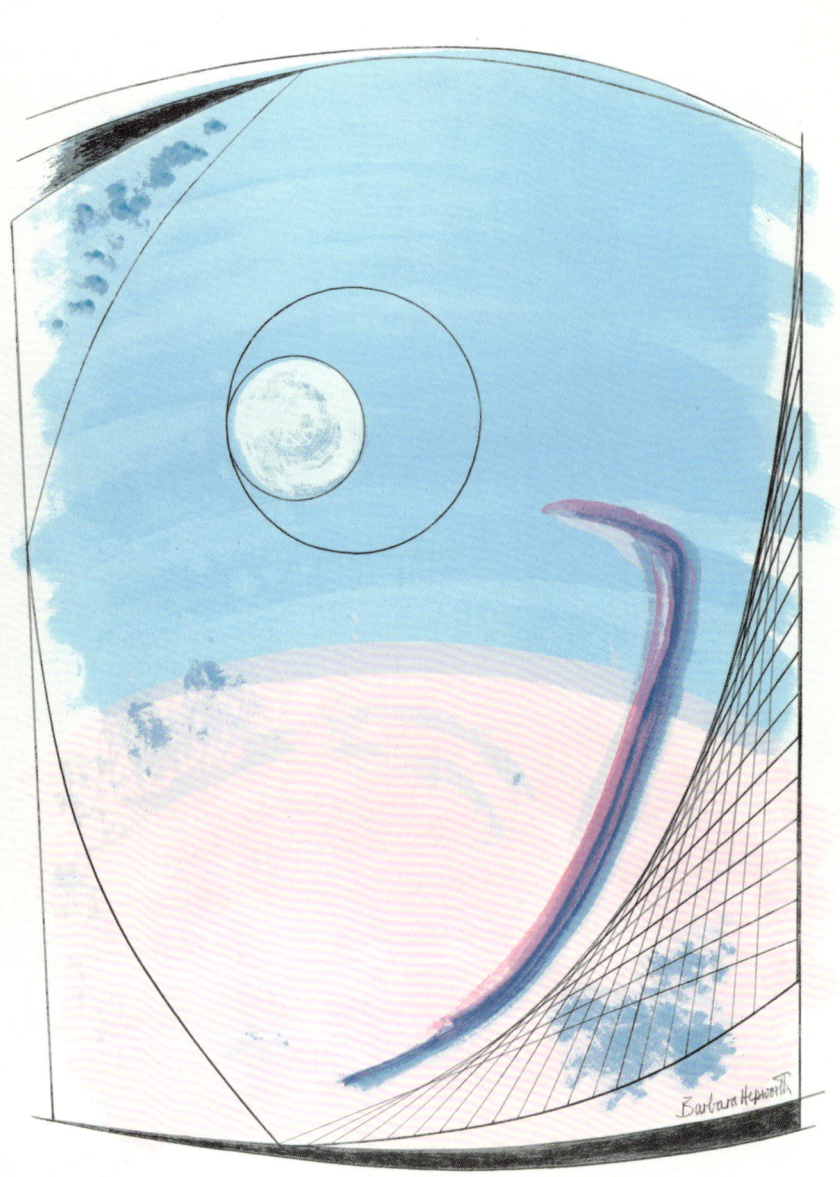

NOTES

1. Quoted in *Barbara Hepworth: Carvings and Drawings*, London 1952, section 1. Reprinted in Sophie Bowness (ed.), *Barbara Hepworth: Writings and Conversations*, London 2015, p.58.

2. Ibid., p.60.

3. Ibid., p.60.

4. *Barbara Hepworth: A Pictorial Autobiography*, Bath 1970, extended 1978 and reprinted by Tate Publishing, 1985, p.17.

5. Hepworth 1952, section 2. Quoted in Bowness (ed.) 2015, p.61.

6. Barbara Hepworth, letter to Ben Nicholson, Sept. 1931, Tate Archive, TGA 8717.1.1.50.

7. Letter from Ben Nicholson to Helen Sutherland, 3 May 1932, Tate Archive. Nicolete Gray loan box 'Correspondence to Helen Sutherland from Ben Nicholson, 1926–1966'.

8. See Lucy Kent, '"An Act of Praise": Religion and the Work of Barbara Hepworth' in *Barbara Hepworth: Sculpture for a Modern World*, exh. cat., Tate Britain, London 2015, pp.37–49.

9. Hepworth 1952, section 2. Quoted in Bowness (ed.) 2015, p.62.

10. Ibid., p.62.

11. Quoted in Sophie Bowness, 'Hepworth and Paris' in *Barbara Hepworth*, exh. cat., Musée Rodin, Paris, 2019, p.34.

12. Penelope Curtis, *British Artists: Barbara Hepworth* (1998), London, 1998 reprint 2013, p.41.

13. Herbert Read, 'Foreword', in *Carvings by Barbara Hepworth, Paintings by Ben Nicholson*, exh. cat., Arthur Tooth &

Sons', London 1932. Quoted in Eleanor Clayton, *Barbara Hepworth: Art & Life*, London 2021, pp.55–6.

14. Hepworth, 1952, section 2. Quoted in Bowness (ed.) 2015, p.61.

15. Ibid., p.64.

16. Ibid., p.64.

17. Quoted in Bowness, 2019, p.35.

18. Bowness (ed.) 2015, p.64.

19. Naum Gabo, Leslie Martin and Ben Nicholson (eds.), *Circle: International Survey of Constructive Art*, London 1937, p.116.

20. Barbara Hepworth, letter to E. Hartley Ramsden, undated, likely November 1941, Tate Archive, TGA 9310.1.1.3. In the same letter Hepworth mentions that she has help from their nanny, Kathleen, although this support 'might get whisked away'.

21. Hepworth 1952, section 4. Quoted in Bowness (ed.) 2015, p.68.

22. E. Hartley Ramsden quoted in Clayton 2021, p.140. See also Rachel Smith, 'Figure and Landscape: Barbara Hepworth's Phenomenology of Perception', *Tate Papers*, no.20, Autumn 2013, https://www.tate.org.uk/research/tate-papers/20/figure-and-landscape-barbara-hepworths-phenomenology-of-perception, accessed 1 Feb. 2024.

23. Quoted in Lyrica Taylor, 'Barbara Hepworth and War' in Dana Cooper and Claire Phelan (eds.), *Motherhood and War: International Perspectives*, New York 2014, p.148.

24. Quoted in Matthew Gale and Chris Stephens (eds.),

Barbara Hepworth: Works in the Tate Collection and the Barbara Hepworth Museum St Ives, London 2001, p.83.

25. Quoted in Sophie Bowness, 'Barbara Hepworth: Artist in Society 1948–53', exh. guide, St Albans Museum and Gallery 2019, unpaginated.

26. Hepworth, 1970, p.52.

27. *Barbara Hepworth: A Retrospective Exhibition of Carvings and Drawings from 1927 to 1954*, Whitechapel Art Gallery exh. cat., texts by Hepworth, section VI. Reprinted in Bowness (ed.) 2015, p.97.

28. Hepworth 1970, p.73.

29. See Stephen Feeke, *Hepworth and the Tache: Drawings and Paintings 1957–58*, paper delivered 12–13 March 2020, Hepworth Research Network Papers.

30. Dag Hammarskjöld, letter to Barbara Hepworth, 16 Oct. 1959, Tate Archive, TGA 20132/2/1/5/6. Quoted in Clayton 2012, p.222.

31. I am grateful to Sophie Bowness for drawing attention to this statement. Originally quoted in Ann Hills, 'The Shapes are Beautiful' in *In Britain*, London, vol. 30, no.9, Sept 1975, p 21.

32. See Katy Deepwell, 'Hepworth and her Critics' in Katy Deepwell (ed.), *Women Artists and Modernism*, Manchester 1998, pp.97–111.

33. Quoted in Curtis 2013, p.91.

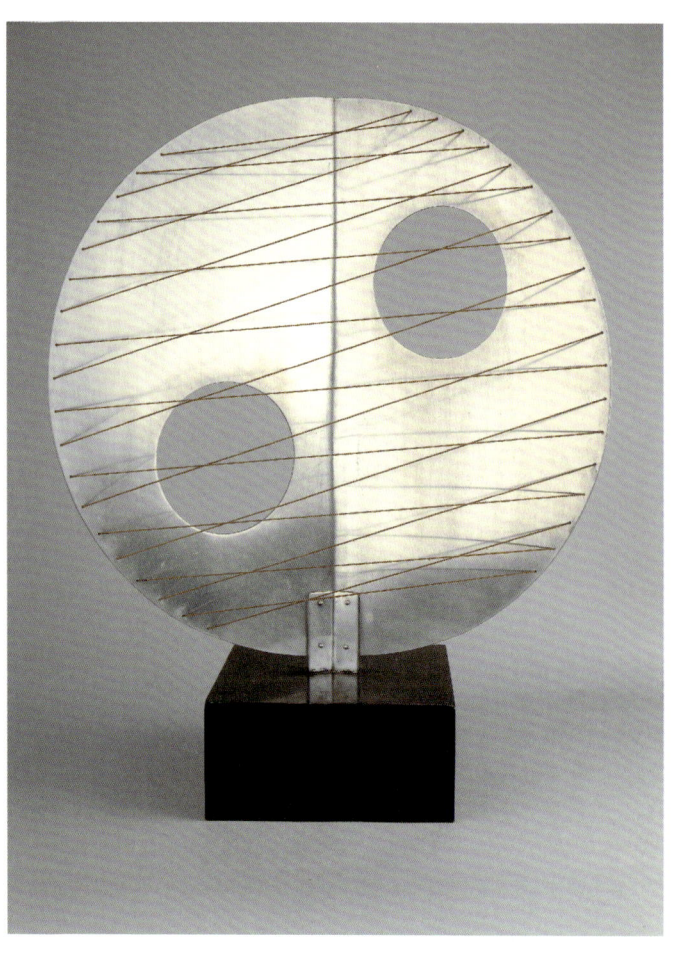

Winter Solstice (Opposing Forms
suite) 1970
Screenprint on paper
77.4 × 58.5

Disc with Strings (Moon) 1969
Aluminium and strings
48.2 × 46.5 × 18

FURTHER READING

Penelope Curtis and Chris Stephens (eds.), *Barbara Hepworth: Sculpture for a Modern World*, exh. cat., London: Tate Publishing 2015

Sophie Bowness (ed.), *Barbara Hepworth: Writings and Conversations*, London: Tate Publishing 2015

Sophie Bowness (ed.), *Barbara Hepworth: The Plasters – The Gift to Wakefield*, Farnham and Burlington: Lund Humphries 2011

Sophie Bowness, *Barbara Hepworth: The Sculptor in the Studio*, London: Tate Publishing 2017

Eleanor Clayton, *Barbara Hepworth: Art & Life*, London: Thames and Hudson 2021

Sally Festing, *Barbara Hepworth: A Life of Forms*, Middlesex: Viking Press, 1995

Matthew Gale and Chris Stephens, *Barbara Hepworth: Works in the Tate Collection and the Barbara Hepworth Museum St Ives*, London: Tate Publishing 1999, repr. 2001

Nathaniel Hepburn, *Barbara Hepworth: The Hospital Drawings*, London: Tate Publishing 2012

Anne Middleton Wagner, *Mother Stone: The Vitality of Modern British Sculpture*, London: Yale University Press, 2005

Alan Wilkinson, *The Drawings of Barbara Hepworth*, Farnham and Burlington: Lund Humphries 2015

First published 2024 by order of the Tate Trustees
by Tate Publishing, a division of Tate Enterprises Ltd
Millbank, London SW1P 4RG
www.tate.org.uk/publishing

A catalogue record for this book is available from the
British Library

ISBN 978 1 84976 901 3

Distributed in the United States and Canada by ABRAMS,
New York

Library of Congress Control Number applied for

Senior Editor: Emma Poulter
Production: Bill Jones
Picture Researcher: Emma O'Neill
Designed by Astrid Stavro
Colour reproduction by DL Imaging, London
Printed and bound in Italy by Printer Trento S.r.l

Cover: *Genesis* 1969 (detail, see p.88)
Frontispiece: *Figure for Landscape* 1959–60
Bronze 269.3 × 137 × 74

Measurements of artworks are given in centimetres,
height before width and depth

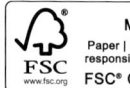

ABOUT THE AUTHOR
Katy Norris is Exhibitions and Displays Curator at Tate
St Ives, and a researcher and writer specialising in women
artists, feminism and social reform movements in Britain
during the early twentieth century. She formerly held the
position of Curator at Pallant House Gallery where she
devised collection displays and temporary exhibitions.
She has worked as advisor for the **Modern Women
Artists** book series published by Eiderdown Books and
has contributed her research to the British Art Network's
Women Artists Subgroup.